To Connie

Going For The Gold

The Complete Guide for Job Hunting and Career Advancement

Darrell Laughlin

Bloomington, IN  Milton Keynes, UK

authorHOUSE®

AuthorHouse™
1663 Liberty Drive, Suite 200
Bloomington, IN 47403
www.authorhouse.com
Phone: 1-800-839-8640

AuthorHouse™ UK Ltd.
500 Avebury Boulevard
Central Milton Keynes, MK9 2BE
www.authorhouse.co.uk
Phone: 08001974150

First published by AuthorHouse 2/16/2008

ISBN: 1-4208-6398-3 (sc)

Printed in the United States of America
Bloomington, Indiana

This book is printed on acid-free paper.

BELIEVE, ACHIEVE & SUCCEED
The danger of NEGATIVE THINKING

Thoughts have a power: positive thoughts do, and negative thoughts do and because thoughts have a way of manifesting themselves in your life, you've Got to be careful what kind of thoughts you entertain. You literally will CREATE in your life what you think. Remember the old adage: You attract unto yourself the equivalent of that which you express. In other words, you bring about what you think and say.

When your thoughts are focused on believing in yourself, on achieving your goals, and imagining success, your subconscious mind will direct your conscious mind and body toward that goal.

In fact nothing else is possible.

If something is not working, change it. Start using your creative mind in developing new ways, better ways. Broaden your visions, broaden your market. If your not making progress, do something about it. Quit listening to somebody else's failures and quit talking about yours. Failure is just a word until you admit it and believe it.

This is a truth, and it is the working principle behind winning. When you desire a thing-that is, when you consciously and seriously set a goal to accomplish something that is humanly possible – Your subconscious mind goes to work to find a way to achieve it. This is written for people who are on the verge of giving up, or about making a career decision. For you Quitting cannot be an option but success in your career search can.

Going for the Gold
Table of Contents

Appendix Worksheets and Forms

Professional Comments

"**Going for the Gold**" - this book is right on dead center! A well-written motivational career guide that is a must for those who are employed and unfulfilled, or out of work and looking for a career. This book is produced out of experience from a successful person and will be of inestimable help for any reader who really wants to do more with their career. Such a book has power - the power to communicate innovative ideals, the power to change attitude and the power to stimulate the will to personal achievement with a successful career.

In my opinion this book will become a classic guide for employment for those of all ages either looking for a career change, re-entering the market, fresh out of school, or for those who just can't seem to get that second interview. But more important is the author, a living example of ideas developed in the book. He writes only what he believes.

John Haley
President
Executone Wireless

I found "**Going for the Gold**" to be an insightful, informative, and valuable read. Laughlin's book is a tremendous asset for individuals seeking employment, especially in today's global economy where every advantage must be utilized to further ones career. His vast experience as a professional coach and recruiter is shared in an easy to use, practical approach.

Patrick B. McCollum
Director Human Resources
PGI Inc.

Going for the Gold" covers all the basics. A straight forward, how-to approach for conducting a job search from beginning to end. This is not a book on how to just write a resume and answer interviewing questions, but presents a perspective of the job search process from the viewpoints of the candidate, employer and professional recruiter. Well worth reading.

Richard E. Phillips
Vice President, Human Resources (ret)
Dayton Walther Corporation

One of life's most formidable challenges is conducting an effective and successful job search. This coupled with the changing economy which requires multiple job searches in most careers makes a source such as Darrell Laughlin's **"Going for the Gold"** more valuable than most other reference guides.

It combines insight gained from experience as an executive recruiter with practical, down to earth recommendations that provide assistance to anyone who reads this guide.

I highly recommend this book to students, graduates, and anyone who is seeking to make a career change or conducting a job search.

John P. Nester
Manager, Human Resources
ESCO Corporation

Acknowledgements

First of all, I wish to thank my beloved mother, Margaret Laughlin who through all of my trials and tribulations stayed steadfast in her devotion to her one and only son, and to my sister, Lynett Wells, for all of her help and kind words of encouragement.

My sincere thanks to my son, Darrell, and his lovely wife, Michele, who had the laborious job of editing and organizing the preliminary manuscript.

I would also like to give special thanks to Linda Matias, President of CareerStrides, who kindly allowed me to use her two articles titled: Three Steps to Writing Resumes and Writing Effective Cover Letters, and who provided me with samples. Her website address is www.careerstrides. com. Mr. Rich Heintz, editor of the California Job Journal for allowing me to use their informative article on unusual questions "What Would I Find in Your Fridge?" Their e-mail address is www.jobjournal.com. Dr. William Melchoir, for helping me with *Communication for Career Success*, and to David Wood with www.solutionbox.com for his quiz on goal setting.

My appreciation to Jim Hargan, a loyal friend who offered me encouragement and suggestions throughout the process of my writing.

Finally, my sincere thanks to Brian Tracy and his organization for letting me use his inspirational quotes from the book, Treasury of Quotes published by yoursuccessstore.com.

Cover Design By: *Derik Lolli*

Going for the Gold

Introduction

"Think continually about what you want, not about what you fear."
Brian Tracy

This book is written for anyone who has lost his or her job due to downsizing, layoffs, plant closings, position elimination, those just starting out in the job market, or individuals looking for a change of career. I am offering you my experience and expertise so that you can become more knowledgeable and successful in conducting your own job search.

You may be asking yourself "Who is Darrell Laughlin, and who is he to write a book on job hunting?" That's a fair question so let me take the time to tell you a little about myself. I have been an active independent corporate recruiter for the past twenty-seven years, matching qualified candidates with administrative, engineering, and executive level positions with companies all across the United States. I have worked with many of the nations top fortune 500 companies, which has given me insight into the essential qualities that these employers are seeking. Following their high standards, I have personally trained over 360 men and women in the course of my career to become professionals in the recruiting field. Several sororities and fraternities have invited me to work with their members to conduct seminars giving them the tools they need in their job searches, whether they be fresh college graduates or alumni interested in a career change. Twenty-seven years of experience has provided me with the necessary qualifications to give guidance and instruction and to assist you in sharpening your skills in order to conduct your personal job search.

Normally, we recruiters are not affected by regional slowdowns in job openings as we typically work on a national level. Due to the cyclical nature of the job market, however, employment rates increase and decrease depending upon market conditions. Usually, what causes job growth to be slow in Michigan, for example, does not affect the job market in let's say, Texas. However, in today's job market, we're beginning to realize a slowing of the economy. The U.S. Department of Labor tells us that our economy has lost over 2.8 million jobs in the past four years. These lost jobs are not temporary layoffs or suspension of business, but are jobs that have been permanently eliminated from our economy. Many of these jobs have gone to foreign competitors, or companies that have relocated their operations abroad. With this in mind, regardless of market outlook, utilizing the job seach techniques as outlined in this book will give you an advantage in locating and securing your job opportunity.

Recent compiled statistics indicate that close to seventy-five percent of people currently holding positions are dissatisfied with their current job situation. The reason for this are lack of promotional opportunites, low salaries, job climate, and disenchantment of what they are currently doing. As a result, many Americans are constantly searching for job opportunites offering their career goals. I personally receive many unsolicited resumes on a weekly basis and many millions post their resumes on online job search boards. Professional recruiters use their own contacts and industry know-how to search for the best man or woman to fill a position. We do not request or expect job seekers to send us their resumes unless their background is pertinent to a job search that we are presently conducting. When you blindly send an unsolicited resume to any firm, you are disregarding the process of corporate recruiting. Take it from me, looking for employment has never been easy, and with the apparent slowing of today's job market, we might expect even more trying times ahead of us. It appears to me that the great economic times and job growth conditions that we had experienced in the past may take several years or more to duplicate. That is why you need to take matters into your own hands and fully take charge of your own job search. Learn to open up the hidden job market where eighty-five percent of the job opportunities lie. Implement the same techniques that we recruiters use to make contacts, initiate introductions, and secure interviews to meet the right people who will actually be qualified to receive your resume and make hiring decisions.

Finding the Motivation You Need for Your Job Search

"Optimism is the one quality more associated with success and happiness than any other." – Brian Tracy

Our thoughts, both negative and positive, have the power over the goals we set and how we work to achieve them. Negative thinking is dangerous! You have to be careful what kind of thoughts you entertain because thoughts have a way of directly and indirectly manifesting themselves into your life. Literally, you will CREATE in your life what you THINK! Remember the old adage, "You attract unto yourself the equivalent of that which you express." In other words, you bring about what you think and say.

When your thoughts are focused on believing in yourself, achieving your goals, and imagining success, your subconscious mind will direct your conscious mind and body toward that goal. In fact, nothing else is possible. Generate a list in your mind of your skills and accomplishments. Be honest with yourself. You have worked hard, made professional improvements, seen your suggestions implemented in your company, and earned promotions.

Set your goals based on your strengths and abilities, and create a plan to work in accomplishing these goals. Do not dwell on failures and other issues of the past. If well-meaning family and friends are negative or pessimistic, you may have to distance yourself from them. The poor attitude of others should not undermine your efforts to achieve your goals and be successful. Listening to someone else's complaints about failures and talking about your own failures is counter-productive. Failure is just a state of mind. When you dwell on the failures of the past, your thoughts will affect your attitude and you will not have the confidence you need to achieve.

If you are not making progress, do something about it. If the methods used in the past to reach your goals have not worked, then it is time to change them. Use your creative mind to develop new and better ways to achieve your goals. For instance, broaden your vision and/or broaden your market.

When you desire a thing, or when you consciously and seriously set a goal to attain something that is humanly possible, your subconscious mind goes to work to find a way to achieve it. This is the principal behind WINNING!

Through my experience, I have been able to identify four key traits exhibited by successful job seekers. Make these traits your own and use them in your job search.

o **Job Seekers Who are Persistent:**
Successful job seekers are the ones that are will-focused and persistent in getting the results they want. They learn to build trust through contacts, job leads, and interviews. Successful seekers do not wait for people to call them. Successful seekers learn how to follow through after the interview and pursue hiring managers without offending them.

o **Job Seekers Who are Motivated:**
The motivated person's goal is to be successful. They are usually competitive and want to WIN. They stay focused on their objective by using a plan they have created on their own. Successful job seekers do not let anyone or anything stop them from winning.

o **Job Seekers Who are Caught Up:**
Serious job seekers stay current on the techniques, tools, and news of their trade. If they are considering employment in a new field, they research their new industry thoroughly. They do not allow themselves to become out of touch with business trends and industry changes. They visit the library or use the internet at least once a week to acquaint themselves with the latest

information and industry changes. They use official web sites to stay up to date on current events in their part of the business world. Successful job seekers routinely skim job advertisements looking for new or different requirements in their field.

o **Job Seekers Who are Responsible:**
Too many times people look for excuses for their failures or settle for mediocre performance from themselves. Responsible job seekers know their strengths and weaknesses. They are honest with themselves and use their own insight and the insight of colleagues to examine their own capabilities and qualifications. They work to improve any factors that might have played a part in their recent job loss. Successful job seekers highlight their strengths as an asset to potential employers.

You are to become your own professional recruiter. To really inspire yourself, write your own credo. Describe your goals and highlight your strengths that you will employ to achieve your goals. This is a personal and private text that you do not need to share with anyone else if you do not wish to divulge it.

Below is an example of my personal philosophy. I wrote this more for myself than for anyone else. It was during a difficult period of my life when problems seemed insurmountable. I needed something to give me the courage and determination to never give up. All difficulties can be overcome with enough will and positive action. As a result, I wrote this and I keep it framed on my desk to always remind me of my goals and the things that I want to achieve. It helps.

> "I hereby resolve to believe upon my strength of determination, to overcome any barriers that may come my way, and to achieve what I set out to achieve. My success is dependent upon how and what I think and what I do. I realize that the road to success is an uphill climb, skewed with many obstacles to test my will and resolve, but I have chosen this path and failure cannot become an option nor deter my goals. The road that I have chosen begins with me and ends with me. I will do what must be done and face any problems with determination and courage. My will must be strong, my desires great, and then I will climb my mountain and raise my eyes to the stars and salute the banner of SUCCESS for I have overcome." -Darrell Laughlin-

Notes

Why Goal Setting

We all need lots of powerful long range goals to help us past the short term obstacles.

Jim Rohn.

Why goal setting? Goal setting is a very powerful method that can result in achieving strong returns in all areas of your life, either personal or career wise. It has been proven that by setting goals you are able to:

- Achieve more
- Increase the motivation to achieve
- Improve self-confidence
- Eliminate negative attitudes that hold you back

Goal setting helps self-confidence. Research has shown that people who incorporate goal setting in their lives:

- Concentrate more
- Perform better at tasks
- Suffer less from stress and anxiety
- Are happier and more satisfied

I have included this quiz to assist you in recognizing and establishing your own personal goals. Please take the time to complete the quiz as it will help you in establishing your goals and identifying your personal priorities.

    A. Rate Your Life:

       How would you rate your life on a scale from one to ten (with ten being that you cannot imagine it any better) in the following areas?

_____Health & Peace _____Money _____Relationship with Partner

_____Family _____Career _____Other (Spirituality)

 Given these results, which 2-3 areas are you most willing to improve over the next 6 months to make the biggest difference to your life?

_____Health & Peace _____Money _____Relationship with Partner
_____ Family _____Career _____Other (Spirituality)

 What three areas are you most *tolerating or putting up* with in your life?

_____Health & Peace _____Money _____Relationship with Partner

_____Family _____Career _____Other (Spirituality)

 What three things do you appreciate most in your life?

_____Health & Peace _____Money _____Relationship with Partner
_____Family _____Career _____Other (Spirituality)

 Of these areas, which one do you desire to have the most in your life?

_____

B. Create your goals:

 Write your goals out in complete detail and set them high enough to challenge yourself. Even if you do not reach the standard that you have set for yourself, everything that you do accomplish will make you a better person. The most important thing is to write down your goals, this becomes your daily guide and sets the process in motion. You must focus on your goals continuously, as this will better enable you to accomplish your objectives.

1) Create 2-3 goals which would make a big difference to your life, put a big smile on your face, and be achievable within 6 months.

Goal: Achieve By:

a)_____   Date:_____

_____

_____

b)_____   Date:_____

_____

_____

c)_____   Date:_____

_____

_____

2) Imagine 6 months have passed and you have succeeded in achieving each of these goals. Write down how you would feel having achieved each one of these.

Goal: I would feel:

a)_____   _____

_____   _____

b)_____   _____

_____   _____

c)_____   _____

_____   _____

If you find that you would not feel as satisfied about each of these as originally thought, then you might like to go back to step 1) and consider bigger or more thoughtful goals.

C.   Shooting Yourself in the Foot:

> 3) Assuming that all human beings have some way of holding back or sabotaging their life, which of the choices listed below is your *favorite* method. This will help you to identify the dominant factor in limiting your success. (choose one only)

__Procrastination   __Indecisiveness   __Arrogance/always being right

__ Acting as "Lone Ranger"   __Tolerance   __Negative attitude

__Controlled by life/ people   __Not saying "Yes"   __Not saying "No"

Following secondary goals (Goals that ultimately will not make me happy)

Deceit (Not always telling absolute truth)

Setting goals, and measuring their achievement, gives you an opportunity to observe what you have done and what you are capable of doing. It will also give you the confidence that you need to achieve higher and more difficult goals.

Review your goals on a daily bases, this is a crucial part of your success and must become part of your routine. Each day when you wake up, read your list of goals and picture in your mind the completed goal. Then each night before going to bed, repeat this process. This will start your sub-conscious and conscious mind on working towards the successful completion of your goals. Someone once stated that "By not setting goals, life is like a ship without a rudder, it just goes around in circles."

Quiz created and compliled by David Wood, a Certified Career Coach at SolutionBox.com.

Notes

Power Questions

If you have ever wanted to really take control of your life, but did not know how or where to begin, then consider utilizing the following questions. These questions may steer you in the right direction or assist you in achieving your desired results in your business career and social life.

Defining Your Goals:

1. If you were to **fully** live your life, what change(s) would you make first?
2. Which areas of your life could be upgraded or "tweaked"?
3. What could you work on now that would make the biggest difference to your life?
4. What are you tolerating or "putting up" with?
5. What would you like **more** of in your life? (Make a list)
6. What would you like **less** of in your life? (Make a list)
7. What three things are you doing regularly that do not serve or support you?
8. How could you make this goal more specific or measurable?
9. What aspect of your life would receive the biggest impact from achieving your goals?
10. What would you attempt to accomplish now if you knew that you could not fail?
11. What do you love?
12. What do you hate?
13. What is the one thing that you would love to do before you pass away?
14. Is now the right time for you to make a commitment to achieving these goals?
15. What could you work on right now that would really put a smile on your face?
16. For your life to be more fulfilling, what would you have to change?
17. What do you really want?
18. What is one change that you could make to your lifestyle that would give you more peace?

Creating an Action Plan:

1. What is the first/next step you need to make to move toward your goal?
2. What research could you do to help you find the first or next step?
3. Who could you talk to who would enlighten you on this issue?
4. Who should you be associating yourself with, so that achieving this goal becomes a natural? (i.e. who is already doing it?)
5. How can you acquire the knowledge/information that you need?
6. What are three actions that you could take that would make sense this week?
7. On a scale of 1 to 10, how excited would you feel about taking these actions?
8. What would increase that score? (I.e. handle fear, clearer steps, more support, or more fun)
9. What will happen (what is the cost) of you **not** doing anything?

New Perspectives to Consider:

1. What can you learn from this?
2. In what way is your current situation absolutely perfect?
3. How could you turn your life around immediately, and enjoy the process?
4. What are you doing well? What could you do better?
5. What is one way that you could have more fun in your life?
6. What is the value of your current attitude?
7. What is your favorite way of sabotaging yourself, and your goals?

Diagnostic Questions:

1. What are three of your greatest strengths?
2. What are you most excited about now? What are you most looking forward to?
3. What is one way to get more energy into your life?
4. What would be your ideal choice for a career if you could choose anything?
5. What is the one thing that you could do to give yourself more peace financially?

6. What do you see as your life is really about? What is your purpose?
7. If you had to guess your life's purpose (from looking at your life to date), what would it be?
8. So far in your life what would you like most to be acknowledged for?

Notes

The Traditional Methods

"Spend eighty percent of your time focusing on the opportunities of tomorrow rather than the problems of yesterday." – Brian Tracy

If you are one of the millions of Americans who have recently lost their jobs, you are probably going through the initial state of shock. You were a loyal, conscientious worker, well-trained with solid experience. Your company had to make reductions and your position became a casualty. Even if you are currently employed you might fear that due to industry trends or recent company history your position or department might soon be targeted for cutbacks. You are not out of a job yet, but you could be very soon.

Your first instinct might be to revise your resume and start sending it to everyone you can possibly think of, responding to every newspaper ad, and submitting it to every internet job-site, anxiously hopeful that your qualifications will be spotted and that some business or corporation has an open position that you could fill. Avoid the mistakes made by many job seekers whose resumes end up with the hundreds of unsolicited resumes received every day in personnel offices across the country. Unfortunately, many hard-working people's resumes end up either being thrown away or put into a database and soon forgotten.

Three commonly used methods of job searching are looking through newspaper classified advertisements, searching the internet's various employment sites, or contacting a corporate recruiter. Although a small percentage of people are successful using these three methods, most are not. I will provide you with the tools you will need to take charge of your own job search. You will use your learned skills to take the initiative and discover job openings before your competitors know of them. After reviewing the traditional methods of job searching, I will inform you as to how we corporate recruiters, and most of the business world, **fill** positions.

First, consider the newspaper classified ads. In the old days newspapers were the chosen format to connect employers with job seekers. Employers would post their job openings and select from those who would reply. Sunday's classified section was the bulkiest, usually more than a dozen pages thick. Classified advertisements are getting thinner and thinner today. Newspapers have to compete with web sites and internet job posting boards for employer's advertisements, and with today's competitive job market, and an over-abundance of job seekers, employers hesitate to advertise job openings for fear of receiving a flood of resumes for just a few select positions.

Secondly, you may wonder, if employers are not advertising in print newspapers, are they then advertising on the internet? In the twenty-first century, we rely more and more on the internet as a medium for research and communication. However, in my professional opinion internet job boards are generally a waste of time and energy. Many jobs listed on job boards are simply out of date. They remain on these sites months after they have been posted and often fail to include a company name, phone number or contact name. You respond either directly to the job board, to an e-mail address, or to a fax number of the unnamed company. You really have no idea where your resume is going or who is reading it. You are better off submitting resumes directly through company websites. At least you will know what business is reading your resume, although you still will not know what person. The truth is that job searches conducted exclusively on-line rarely produces results.

Here is some information that should open your eyes as to how effective internet job searching really is. The Wall Street Journal reported that the percentage of hires recently made by using the four biggest job boards are Monster.com which produced 1.4% of new employees. Hotjobs.com was much less successful, recruiting only.39% of new employees while only .29% of positions were filled through Career Builder.com. Finally .27% of jobs were filled through Headhunter.net. The combined total employment power of these four job search sites is only 2.35% of all new hires! Therefore, based on this information, you should not solely depend on using job boards as a means to finding employment.

In a further recent poll, employers reported that they use non-company internet sites, including job boards, to recruit and fill only 8% of their job openings. Even company web sites were not very successful. In 2004, only 16% of new hires were as a direct result of people submitting their resumes to corporate web sites. Many of these successful candidates improved their chances of being interviewed by naming personal contacts within the company when applying. Yes, employers used their own company websites and internet job boards to fill a total of 24% of their open positions, but they also reported that many positions were filled by candidates who did not submit a resume or application on-line. From the job seeker's standpoint, the results were equally disappointing. Included in the poll, it was reported that only 4% of candidates questioned found their jobs on the internet. The poor results of on-line and newspaper classified employment matches is pretty grim news for today's job seeker. Believe it or not the best jobs do not get advertised at all, and most employment openings are never posted online or otherwise advertised. If you really want to find employment, develop your **networking skills**. Networking is the secret to job finding and allows you to tap into the "hidden" job market where 85% of jobs are filled.

You are a top-quality candidate and some employer is in need of your skills and expertise. By applying the techniques that you are going to learn, you will be able to find your job using methods tried and trusted in the corporate world.

In today's market, employers trying to fill a position are currently being deluged with an over-abundance of resumes from their job postings. Consequently, you as a job seeker can expect the volume of competition to be out of sight. It is easy using internet technology to broadcast your generic resume or to be one of the hundreds to respond to a job listing. This is why employers are reluctant to advertise job openings for fear of the flood of resumes that they will receive in response. If you really want results, you need to find out about employment needs that are not advertised. Job- hunting is going to take much work and effort on your part. The sooner you realize this, the better off you will be.

Another mistake job seekers make is blindly sending off their resumes to corporate recruiters. As a recruiter, the last thing I need is more non-solicited resumes. Companies contract me to search for candidates with the precise qualifications to obtain an available position in their company. We are called "headhunters" because we are hunting for a very specific type of individual to fulfill our client's needs. We use our own contact methods and connections to initiate our search. We do not have the time or the energy to read every resume that we receive. Your resume will most likely end up in a pile with all of the other over-looked resumes we receive or delete from our e-mail.

In the corporate recruiting world, we refer to unsolicited resumes as "mass mailings." Someone who prints up eighty copies of their resume and either sends it to every business in the phone book that is remotely related to their field, or e-mails it to every recruiter listed in a directory with the hope of getting called. As a recruiter, I do not need these resumes, so why would an employer? One day I was on the phone with a client, a major corporate executive, when he said, "Listen to this"...CLUNK! I asked him what made that noise and he responded that it was a stack of resumes that he had collected over the last several days making their way to the trashcan. I then asked him if he had reviewed any of them. He answered, "No." He indicated that he didn't have the time to review every resume that he received.

In essence, do not become too excited about mass mailing your resume to a multitude of companies. It is a proven fact that you should only expect a response from 2% of the employers who were sent an unsolicited resume, and most of the time, it is just to inform you that they had received your resume. Given this statistic, can you imagine how many resumes are in circulation in today's job market and how many remain unnoticed?

The U.S. Department of Labor suggests several sources in reference to learning about job openings. Remember, the vast majority of employment opportunities are never listed with any of these sources. However, the list may be very useful in providing ideas for places where you can make additional contacts and begin to enhance your personal employment database.

Where to Learn About Job Openings

1. **Personal contacts.**
2. School career planning and placement offices.
3. Classified advertisements in national and local newspapers, professional journals and trade magazines.
4. Internet networks and resources.
5. State employment service offices.
6. Federal government employment service offices.
7. Professional associations.
8. Labor unions.
9. Private employment agencies and career consultants.
10. Community agencies.

Notes

How to Respond to Job Advertisements

In the occurrence that you come across an employment ad, in either a newspaper or magazine, which you feel that you would be qualified for or have an interest in exploring, my advice is that you wait at least five to seven days before submitting your resume and cover letter. This delay will help in preventing your information from being rejected simply because the screener is reviewing the initial volume of responses that typically collects within the first two or three days after the ad runs.

In most cases, the best style of cover letter to use in responding to a newspaper ad is a comparison style, which *clearly* compares the job requirements to your own qualifications. This will help steer the screener, who may not posses a great deal of experience or knowledge especially in the technical nature of the job, toward a more favorable assessment of you.

Many ads will also request a salary history or requirement. This is the most convenient information that you can supply to eliminate you as a viable candidate. If you state a salary range that is higher or lower than the usually unpublished salary range authorized for the position, you most likely will not be contacted for the position. My advice to you is to not submit salary information. A recent survey of 159 human resources and "hiring decision makers" nation-wide conducted by the Career Masters Institute and titled " Revealing Trends in Corporate Hiring Practices" indicated that 56 percent of respondents would consider qualified candidates even when they do not provide salary information as requested. Another 31 percent said it depends entirely on the candidate's experience.

Only 11 percent of those surveyed stated that they would not consider the candidate without salary information. Given that you are theoretically marketing and selling your services to potential buyers, keep in mind that a good salesman sells his product first and price last.

Notes

Comparison Letter

Contact Name, Title
Company
Address
City, State. zip

Dear_____

Your advertisement for a (position title) caught my interest. It appears that you are offering an exciting opportunity for the right individual – and I feel I am that person. During my (no.) years in the (occupational) field, I have had a number of accomplishments in which you may be interested. In fact, they seem to be an excellent match for your position.

Skills required: My qualifications:

   1.   1.
   2.   2.
   3.   3.

I would welcome the opportunity to meet with you, learn more about the specifics of this position, and discuss the ways in which I believe I can meet them. I will submit a salary history and other personal information at such time as you indicate serious interest in my qualifications.

Please give me a call so that we can arrange a time to meet at your convenience.

Sincerely,

Name

Encl: resume

Notes

Networking

If you recall from the previous section, most decent jobs do not get advertised in newspapers, put on job boards, or even listed on company websites. Therefore, you may ask, how do managers fill open positions? Simple...they depend on in-house referrals. It has been estimated that 85% of all jobs are obtained by either word of mouth or employee referrals. Actually, many companies offer their employees a referral fee for successfully recruiting an individual for a particular position. These fees may run as high as $1000 for each referred candidate who is hired. A pretty good company incentive, don't you think? In fact, you may be wondering how you might become involved with this method. Please allow me to open your eyes to the numerous possibilities.

Career consulting businesses charge a large amount of money to assist you with resume and cover letter writing, as well as to teach you to develop the necessary networking skills to facilitate this process. I will be giving you all of these tools for just the price paid for this book. What does networking do for you? Networking is a powerful means in which to land a job. For starters, it eliminates competition so you have a greater chance of getting a job. It also broadens your knowledge of the local market and enlarges your contact base. All professional recruiters use the networking system. It is the most effective and efficient way of locating the type of individual our client needs. Furthermore, it works! Throughout this process, we maintain a database of contacts and we are always asking the same question, "Whom do we know?"

You begin this process by making up a "list". I call it a "list" but what you are really creating is a database for all of your information about personal contacts, industry trends, specific companies, and known job openings. Your job right now is to promote yourself in the same format for all of your notes so that you can efficiently compare your information on the different contacts or various companies.

Perhaps, you will want to create a spreadsheet for all of the collected data. Your resumes will be included in this file. Resume writing will be discussed in a later chapter.

Remember, it is who you know (contacts), what you know (current knowledge regarding the industry trends) and where you know (specific company names). Use your contacts to stay up to date on industry trends and learn the names of other companies and people that you might contact. Use your knowledge gained of the industry to determine who you need to know and which companies are the most interesting and promising to you. Use your familiarity of each company to identify department managers and stay current on industry news.

Company Names

First of all, take inventory of your skills and accomplishments. This by far is the most important. Be honest with yourself. Note all of your improvements, promotions, and cost-saving suggestions that were implemented by previous employers. As you work on the search, continue to add items to this list, as well as refine it. You will need this information during your initial phone calls, while creating your resume/ cover letter, and throughout the interviewing process.

Having begun on a positive note with listing your accomplishments, start gathering the vital information that you will need to know in order to promote yourself. Begin your database by listing the specific companies for whom you would like to work for in the future. List all of the details that you may already know about the company, such as department managers, personal contacts, and recent company news. Do not be overly concerned if you have limited information in the beginning of this process. Your task will be to gather all the needed data. Remember to include in your notes why you chose each company. For example, does the company have a reputation for being fair and honest with their customers and employees? Is the company a leader in the industry?

After listing all of the companies that you would be interested in working for, continue to expand your list by including your previous employer's competitors and suppliers for they may be in need of your services. Being that you are already familiar with their industry and operations, it may be worth your while to contact them. Add these companies to your list. Also, research these companies further and identify additional contact names.

A good resource for increasing your network is the local chapter of the professional association for your field of interest. Refer to the website of the American Society of Association Executives, found at www.asaenet.org. This website will assist you in your search for an appropriate affiliation and help you gather more names of companies in regions within the United States where you would like to work.

If your field does not have a professional association, begin by making a list of whom you know in your field. List even those people with whom you are not well acquainted. Next, call and visit each colleague and observe his or her work environment. Note the skills that are required, the chain of command, which departments are related to the person you are visiting, and any other pertinent information. Ask if he or she knows of any job openings in either their company or another for which you might apply. For each company a colleague suggests, ask for the name and phone number of a possible hiring authority. Do not be discouraged if the colleague is hesitant to offer a phone number or contact name. Use your own resources to find the phone number. Also, ask for names and phone numbers of their colleagues and where they work. Introduce yourself to each person suggested. The focus at this point is to keep adding to your contact list. **Always ask permission to use your contact's name before following up on their referrals.** Send each contact a courtesy note thanking them for taking the time to speak with you and to please keep you in mind if any positions were to open within their company.

Another good source for information is to create a list of everyone you know, even if they are not in your industry. Call each of these individuals and find out where they work, what they do, whether they know of any positions that may be available within their own company, who is responsible for hiring, and any other pertinent information to assist in your job search. It does not matter what they do for a living. This could range from being a mechanic to an executive. You may think that this is being redundant but your list needs to include *everyone you know*! You may be surprised as to what you might find. These people are working and know what is going on within their company. Also consider asking whom they know. Continue expanding your different contact lists. Believe me, eventually, it will pay off! This is how jobs are getting filled.

Local and state government offices are other very valuable resources. Whether you are looking for information in your own region or planning to move, government agencies provide vital statistics on businesses in their jurisdiction(s). Definitely contact the Chamber of Commerce within your area. When calling them, request business listings or industrial guides and find out what companies are fairly new to the area and what companies might be expanding. Sometimes you will have to pay a fee for these listings but often, you may be able to receive them at no cost. The staff at the Chamber of Commerce is usually willing to help and you should find them to be a very good resource because they process a large amount of information about local area businesses.

Once you have received the list from the Chamber of Commerce, pick out the businesses that match your industry interests and qualifications. Call these companies to obtain the names and extension numbers of the hiring authority to whom you can forward your resume. Remember, **not** to send your resume until you have spoken directly with the hiring authority.

An additional resource that most people do not consider is your local city hall. Contact the department that issues business licenses and request that they send you the listings of new companies that have applied for or recently have been issued a business license. Once you receive this list pick out those businesses that interest you. These businesses typically are new and in their "start-up" stage. They should need people, right? Do your company research and give them a call!

Another good source is your Secretary of State's office. This office will also give you details about companies in the process of incorporation within the state or a particular region of the state. All of these city and state records are public information and accessible to you. It is imperative that you beat your competition and become the first in line.

Contact Names

The next step in organizing your file is updating your contact list, both business and personal. You should have identified contacts for each and every company on your list. If you do not have a particular business's contact name, check with the company operator and ask for the name of the hiring manager for the department you would like to join. Attempt not to divulge the true motive of your call or that you would like to submit a resume, because normally when this happens you are directed to the personnel department, and that is the one department that you want to stay out of for now. If asked what this is in regards to, just inform them that you would like to forward information to the manager's attention that is pertinent to his area. I have generated a good amount of business by talking directly to department managers and letting them know of qualified candidates that I represent.

As a last resort, get the name of the human resources manager. The human resources personnel are usually aware only of existing department openings, but do not necessarily have insight as to what the department manager is thinking. Managers may be thinking of expanding their departments or replacing underachievers.

Company Information

Do your homework. **Research, Research, and Research** each company's profile. Know what they do and how they do it. What corporations they may belong to. Are they a subsidiary of a larger organization? Have they acquired a smaller company into their own structure? Find out what new products or services the company has introduced and what percentage of the market does the company represent for the products or services it sells. Find out about company growth, recent promotions within the company, and any other useful facts. Utilize the company's official web site and other web sites associated with the industry. Research is where the internet is truly valuable as a gathering tool for information on specific industries, or for individual corporate knowledge. Subscribe to trade publications and use other resources, such as your local library. Use the library to review magazines, business reports, and other research materials. Each company should have its own data sheet in your file.

A Word about Networking

For those of you who say, "networking doesn't work" or "I've tried it and it just didn't work for me", keep in mind you cannot just try it once and expect it to materialize on the first few attempts. Like everything else, you must be persistent to achieve results. Recruiters must become masters at networking or they become very non-productive. Networking is simply exercising good people skills and building strong relationships. Some people may be very hesitant in referring someone to their hiring managers for a job. They must feel comfortable and confident with recommending you for a position. This is where the trust and relationship begins. Do not expect everyone you talk with to extend their reputation just to help you. There is too much at stake. Results should not be expected to happen overnight. Prepare yourself, do your homework, and then receive the results with which you worked hard to achieve.

When creating your referral list, identify the people that you know that would be willing to help you, willing to offer you contacts, and begin from there. People who are convinced that networking does not work are just not working the system. Most people who find work through an outplacement service are using a service schooled in networking. Approximately two-thirds of those positions were filled using this method. It is important to understand that when we are faced with something new in our lives that we all typically experience fear or apprehension. Mostly, it is the fear of change. We want to protect ourselves from possible embarrassment or the chance of failure. This is natural for all of us but you cannot allow yourself to stop because of fear. Concentrate on positive results. Opportunities are waiting for you. You just need to take a step forward. If you are somewhat shy and feel uncomfortable in face-to-face discussions, realize the fact that the person at the other end probably has a lot of the same worries and concerns in life as you do. We are all people and we all have problems. With this in mind, work up an introduction and a short list of questions that you would like answered. Also, it is imperative that you start mixing with business groups in your field, church, or alumni associations to begin developing your networking skills. Walking up to someone and saying something like, "I need a job. Do you know someone who is hiring" is by far the wrong approach. I once observed someone at a business function who did just that and needless to say, he did not receive much feedback.

The fact remains that networking does work! I know because it has worked for me these past 28 years and it will work for you if used correctly.

Notes

Small Businesses

Small businesses have always been the cornerstone for job creation. Research has shown that at least two-thirds of all jobs are from the small business sector. A recent survey conducted by the National Federation of Small Business indicated that since 1999 smaller establishments added more employees than any other sector. In addition, this survey points out that hiring among small business owners should remain fairly robust in the future. It was further reported that 13 percent of those surveyed expect to create new job openings, while slightly more than one-fifth of those firms reported having at least one job opening that was difficult to fill. This information was of no surprise to me. As a recruiter I target small businesses to create new job leads because small businesses normally do not have the resources, such as staff and budgets for attracting critical employees as major firms do.

What constitutes a small business? Normally, it is a business that employs from 2 to 500 individuals and generates sales of $100,000 to $15 million and sometimes more. The service industry comprises the largest percentage of small business with 30.5 percent, followed by the retail industry at 22.6 percent. The construction industry and the manufacturing industry follow behind with 15.9 percent and 11.3 percent, respectively. Small businesses account for 40 percent of our entire gross domestic product.

As far as new job creation and rapid growth opportunities, you should not overlook investigating this area. Think of Microsoft, Apple, Ford Motor Company, and all the other giants that had small business beginnings. I will give you a short story about one small company. During my sister's search for a career some years back, in Cupertino, a small northern California town, her daily route took her past a small ordinary looking building. Working in that building were two young individuals developing a design for a personal computer. Can you guess who they were? Well, if you guessed Apple, you were right.

It is kind of ironic that my sister was out driving, looking for that great opportunity, and was unaware that she was passing by one every day. I sometimes wonder what could have emerged if she had gotten a flat tire in front of that location, asked for their assistance, and had gotten into a discussion about what they were up to. I guess hindsight is twenty/twenty.

My point in sharing this story with you is quite simple. Even though a business may appear small or just in the beginning stages does not mean that unlimited opportunities are not out there waiting for you. In fact, it may be safe to assume that quite the opposite could be expected. Therefore, explore the area in which you live to determine whether or not there are companies near you that could be on the leading edge of technology or other services. You may even want to consider staying current on local business news because you just might find a gem and the start of a fantastic career!

Notes

Leads Generation

Other than receiving leads by employing the previously covered methods, such as the Chamber of Commerce, industrial guides, public libraries, trade associations, newspaper articles, competitors of companies previously worked for and their suppliers, and your own networking efforts, you might also check with your local library for a stock buyers guide such as Standard & Poors and Moody's. Begin searching these guides for companies that interest you and make contact with their Investor's Relations Representative.

While you have the individual on the phone convey to him/her that you are interested in learning about their company and its growth, etc. These people are there to sell you on a stock investment with their company and will give you as much information as you ask. After building a rapport, you can then ask additional questions, such as the name of a department head that you would be interested in making a telephone contact with and hopefully sending a cover letter and resume to that individual. Your original intent was to purchase stock in the company and after your discussion; you are now sold on working with this company! Imagine that! I have seen this method used successfully. This is an especially helpful method for long distance job searching. Keep in mind that this may require making many phone calls and sending numerous letters to make your job search pay off.

Notes

Job Fairs Good or Bad

In my years in the recruiting business, I have attended many job fairs and have even conducted a few myself. What I have discovered is that there are pros and cons to job fairs. Some companies attend these fairs to specifically fill existing needs. While others attend just to add on to their candidate database or to establish a presence.

I have also seen a few people invited to a company's facilities for an in-depth interview. Nevertheless, for many it is just an exercise to see what companies are represented and to submit resumes in the hope that someone may call them at a later date. Some job fairs are well worth attending. However, this often depends upon how well it is organized. When I was responsible for conducting a job fair, I regularly had a team of recruiters who would acquire a copy of a candidate's resume prior to them entering the main room. In addition, these recruiters would question each candidate on the type of position desired, the salary level, and the type of industry that interested them. As a result of this preliminary step in the process, and the fact that we had a list of the positions available within each company, we would either escort the candidate for an introduction to the company's representative or we would direct individuals to specific companies who we felt would have an interest in the candidate's background. Often times, however, these situations were in the minority. Much of the time, we were asked to make copies of each resume and then provide each employer a resume packet for their review.

You might be asking yourself if job fairs are even worth the investment of your time. In answering this question you need to know whether it is a good or bad job fair. The following is an example of a poorly organized job fair. I once was under contract with a major aerospace manufacturer to attend a job fair sponsored by a very large company also in the aerospace field but was down sizing their work force by approximately 13,000 employees, most of which were salaried staff, such as personnel, engineering, research and development etc. Much to my dismay, there were only three companies who represented the aerospace industry. Another firm and I were in attendance while a third firm, that did not attend, just wanted resumes sent to them. The remaining companies in attendance had no idea at all as to the type of positions that these people were looking for. For instance, a couple of the companies were seeking representatives simply to sell insurance, a soft drink company looking for a sales representative, and I even saw a Mary Kay's cosmetics booth. My guess is that the company organizing the job fair just wanted to fill up their available booths. Why these firms were attending a high tech job fair was beyond me. Needless to say, the candidates were very disappointed and I and the other firm went home with over 3,000 resumes to sort through. This particular job fair had to be the worse one that I have ever attended.

Now, I am not stating that all job fairs are bad. In fact, some are very well organized and could end up being quite effective. Therefore, it is really up to you to decide. Attending one will give you a greater opportunity to better expose yourself to the job market and maybe even land a job. If you do decide to participate in a job fair and are approached by a company's representative that you are interested in pursuing, make sure that you introduce yourself and ask questions about the company and what they do rather than just handing them your resume and moving on. You might also want to consider asking them about their industry's standing, expectant growth, and the company's overall potential, as well as questioning them about what they are presently looking for and maybe their knowledge of possible openings in the near future. Using this approach will enable you both to feel more comfortable in exchanging information and will encourage a conversation which might be beneficial to you. Once this groundwork has been set, you can begin sharing your work history and your experience, as well as elaborate on the type of job that you are interested in.

This approach is considered to be an ice- breaker. I have observed far too many individuals just drop off a resume at one booth and move on to another without any dialogue taking place. How they would expect to generate interest on the part of an employer, I'll never know. I realize that with time constraints or in the event that they are tied up talking with another candidate, it may not be possible for you to stop and talk to every company representative that appears interesting to you. However, if a specific company appears particularly interesting then you could take advantage of this time to browse through any of their company literature. This will give you additional information needed for an engaging dialogue.

If you discover in your conversation with a company representative that they do not have a need for the skill you bring to them, then ask them who in attendance might be looking for someone with your type of experience. This is an important question to ask because prior to the start of a job fair, the representatives from the various companies commonly get together and discuss their individual employment needs. Therefore, by asking this question they may just direct you to your potential employer. Always remember to request a business card from the individuals that you talk with. On the back of the card make notations about these individuals and their company so that when you call them or follow up with a thank you letter, you can personalize your comments in regards to your first meeting.

I would not advise traveling a great distance to attend a job fair unless it is specialized within your industry. Also, attending a *trade show* within your industry may prove more beneficial than attending a general job fair. You would be surprised to discover how many resumes are exchanged during these types of events. You might have an excellent opportunity at that time to meet some hiring managers who regularly attend these functions. I would never advise you not to attend a job fair. Ultimately, you will have to weigh the pros and cons of attending before making your decision. Just keep in mind that the more you expose yourself to potential job opportunities the quicker you may become employed.

Notes

Developing
a Letter Campaign

An additional component to the job searching process may include sending a few letters to prospective hiring managers. There may be an advantage to utilizing this step in the process especially if you are finding it difficult to talk with them in person. After creating your list of companies of interest and verifying them by researching the name, title, and business address of the hiring authority, write a handwritten personalized note. Make sure that you use quality paper because your visional presentation is most important in this process.

In your letter summarize your experience and education, adding only the elements that are relevant to the position. Notify the individual that you would like to give them a brief telephone call the following week. In the letter specify a specific day and time frame. For, instance, you might say, "I would like to contact you next Wednesday between 9:00 a.m. and 12:00 p.m. for a few minutes of advice." You might also add that if that particular time is not adequate, you would be happy to contact them at a time more convenient. As a side note: generally the best time to reach them is often just after the regular business hours so be prepared of that availability in time. If you received the hiring manager's name from a referral, make sure that you include the referral's name in the text. The following is an example of what to write.

Dear Mr. Smith:

Sam Johnson, a mutual friend of ours suggested that you might be able to recommend some options for me.

I have a degree in plant accounting with over 7 years of experience and have recently made a decision to actively pursue a career change. Recently, I have been working under a heavy work schedule and have not had the opportunity to learn what may be available in my field. I would appreciate talking with someone with a broader overview of the market in our area.

I would like to call you on Wednesday morning (May 6th) between 9:00 am. and 12:00 p.m. Just so that you understand, I am not requesting employment but only a few minutes for some sound advice in your industry. If I am unable to connect with you at this time, I will call later in the day or later in the week.

Thanking you in advance.

Respectfully,

When addressing the envelope, make sure that you mark it: **Personal and Confidential** to his/her attention. Try to schedule your writing and mailing as well as making your phone calls every day, especially if you are not currently employed. If you are presently employed and your time is limited, write your letters on the weekend and try to make two or three calls just before lunch. If the hiring authority is out, let the operator or secretary know that you will be tied up for awhile and suggest the best time to reach you. Always get the operator or secretary's name and make a note in your company file. These individuals can be your best allies for insight into what is going on within the company.

Notes

Career Changing

"Success in its highest and noblest form calls for peace of mind, enjoyment, and happiness which come only to the man who has found the work that he likes best."

- Napoleon Hill

During the course of their life, many people have considered changing their career fields, either due to personal preference or to instability in their present occupation. In recent years this has been brought forth primarily by the exodus of many jobs to foreign countries and manufacturing plant closings. During my tenure as a recruiter, I have seen numerous individuals change their career fields and become successful in their new chosen field.

If you are having difficulty in finding a position in your field, did not like what you were doing in your past employment or even your present one, then I would advise you to consider making a career change. This may be an excellent opportunity for you to change your life for the better. Studies have shown that the most successful people are in occupations that they enjoy. They are successful simply because they are doing what they like to do. Hence, they are motivated to excel moreover than those that are not satisfied or happy with what they are doing. Making this kind of decision is never easy. Change is always difficult, especially if you have years of experience in another field, but it is possible! The following scenario provides a visualization of what I mean. Being new to the recruiting business many years ago, an older gentleman came into my office and requested that I talk with him about possible employment opportunities. During the course of our interview, he informed me that he had been a senior financial officer for a major corporation and had retired two years previously. He also indicated that he had no particular interest in returning to the financial field, that in the last two years of his position he had felt a total lack of job satisfaction, and was often exhausted by the constant day to day pressures involved. However, he had grown tired of gardening and playing golf and now had a desire to become productive in an occupational setting once again. He stated that he had visited many of the employment agencies and recruiting firms in the area and had left with no tangible leads. Since he had spent most of his career in accounting, he felt at a total loss in regard to career changing at this stage in his life. To be honest with you, I was not sure what to do for him myself, except to ask him more questions relating to what type of position he might be interested in. At this point I was really stumped and wondered how I should proceed. Here is a man with twenty plus years in accounting, retired, wanting to work but not in the area of accounting. While reading his application I noticed that his primary hobby was woodworking. He informed me that he had a complete woodworking shop in his garage with all of the latest equipment. When I asked him what he made, he answered with just about everything from furniture to kitchen cabinets which he designed himself, and had on a part time basis sold them to his neighbors and a couple of small building contractors. You could feel the enthusiasm in his voice as his facial features lit up when he began talking about something he really enjoyed. It was at that precise moment when I thought of a possible job opportunity for him.

I had recently finished an unrelated search assignment for a large woodworking company who manufactured television cabinets for such companies as Sears, Motorola, and RCA. I immediately called my friend who was their Director of Human Resources and gave him a presentation of my candidate. I also explained about this gentleman's retirement status and the reasons that he cited for wanting to re-gain active employment. My friend asked me when he could meet with the candidate and I replied that he was available now. At which point, my friend told me to send him over to the plant immediately. Unfortunately in my excitement, I did not get an actual job description so I could not adequately prepare this gentleman for the interview. However, I gave him a general illustration of the company and sent him away with that bit of limited information. He was pretty excited about being granted an interview on such a short notice, and as he left, I requested that he call me as soon as he finished with the interview.

After about three hours had passed, I received a call from him. He was so choked up and excited that he could barely speak. He told me that the Director of Human Resources had extended him an offer as a cabinet designer and he accepted the position on the spot. Helping this retired gentleman in his search for a new career pleased me more than finding a position for any other individual to this day. The moral of this story attempts to illustrate that becoming aware of and focusing on your passions and interests could be a great place to start in choosing a new career.

If you are presently employed and seriously considering making a career change you should first identify the areas that you dislike in your current employment and see if these can be changed. It may be a matter of simply talking with your boss about your concerns to see if you can resolve the issue(s). Even talking about the possibility of cross training within your company may be a plausible option. You may be surprised where that type of conversation may lead. Progressive companies do not like to lose productive, motivated employees and will sometimes go the extra mile to keep them on board.

However, if you have decided that things cannot be changed and it is time to move on, then I have outlined some suggestions to help you make this transition. First, determine what you would most like to do. In other words, list the type of job, the type of industry, the skills, experience(s), and qualifications as pertaining to your desired occupation. Identify the type of work environment that would best suit your personality and personal needs. In addition, list the skills that you possess that are transferable, as well as the areas of responsibilities that you enjoy. Second, do your homework by researching the field you are interested in pursuing. Read trade magazines or look up trade associations on the internet to gain as much detail as possible about careers that interest you the most. Perform a background study on companies that most interest you in your career goals. Third, determine what type of additional training that you will need in the career that you are exploring based upon the skills that you already possess. Once you have determined the skill(s) that you still need, check into who may be offering this type of training. Remember that all good things begin with a price you must be willing to pay. Fourth, develop a resume that highlights your transferable skills. Although you may not have work experience directly related to your prospective field, it does not mean that you do not have some of the required skills needed for a particular job, identify those refined skills and be confident! Finally, beginning a new career may require taking a cut in salary. Therefore, you should prepare yourself, and if need be, consider it an investment on your future. Keep in mind that the happier you are, the more successful you will become!

There are countless career fields to choose from in an ever-changing business world. Make sure that your expectations are clear and realistic, as well as sincere and obtainable. Let go of your doubts and fears. Many people have done what you are aspiring to do either by choice or necessity, and most have done it successfully just like my cabinet designer.

Notes

Hidden Talents

"To take no risk is the biggest risk of all." – Robert G. Messer

Most people have more talent than the jobs they were hired for, and perhaps every individual has hidden talents that are just not being utilized or developed. I recently read an article indicating that most of today's workers are disenchanted with their present positions primarily because of a lack of development opportunities. While skills and knowledge can be learned, talent is instinctive.

How do we go about developing our hidden talents? For example, if you are presently employed and feel that you have a talent for sales and marketing, ask your employer if it would be possible for you to occasionally sit in on a sales and marketing meeting. Perhaps you have a knack for planning or forecasting possible marketing trends. You could be in the production area and have a talent for recognizing better methods and proficiencies. There are a number of possible areas that you could apply your talents; you just have to discover one and bring it to your employer's attention. If your employer is not interested in your objective, it may be time to move on. If you are going to spend the next 20 to 30 years of your life working, why not do something that will offer you more challenges, career development, and job satisfaction.

Many people go through life unaware as to what their talents are. We all have dreams about how we would like to see ourselves in the future, and think about what we would like to be doing. If you are being somewhat realistic these dreams can be possible, especially when you consider the fact that someone is probably living this same dream. It may require additional education, career changing, or any number of other things. This is strictly up to each individual to decide. Make up a list of what you feel your strengths and talents are, what field of employment most interests you, and how you can apply your talents to this field.

49

Investigate and determine what you must do to make it happen. The opportunities are truly unlimited, especially if you want to explore *or create* new trends.

Keep in mind that more and more people are choosing to work out of their homes, either for an employer or a home-based business that they can build on their own. This will require time, money, and perhaps a great deal of courage on your part. I remember one of my mentors who once said, "Darrell, the fruit doesn't grow on the trunk, you must climb out on the limb to pick it." What he meant to imply is this; often, success requires taking risks at some point in your life.

Notes

Relocating

Bearing in mind that cyclical fluctuations in a given region's economy and job market are not particularly uncommon, many people consider relocation. Maybe the local job market is too depressed or a spouse has gotten an employment opportunity in another city. Perhaps it could also be that you just desire a change of scenery. Now may be a good time to relocate!

If you are wanting and willing to relocate to another location, the best advice that I can give is to select a couple of cities or towns in the area that you are most interested in, and either subscribe to the local newspapers or locate them on-line. Browse the local business section and check out the classified ads. Even though you plan on using the more direct approach to meet potential employers and search for unadvertised positions, knowing what jobs are being advertised will give you some idea as to what is going on in that area. Also, contact the Chamber of Commerce as well as the city and state offices relevant to your desired location and request a copy of their industry directories.

Another suggestion is to make contact with the largest realtor(s) in the area. While discussing housing costs, ask them what they know of the area's employment opportunities. Realtors frequently know what is happening in the local job market and are motivated to help you because of the possible commissions you would bring if you used their office in your housing search.

Many candidates will ask me about the possibility of an employer paying for them to relocate. I inform them that it usually depends on the state of the present economy. In slow economic times most employers typically will not pay the heavy cost of relocating new hires. Although there are employers who would be willing to pick up relocation expenses, they usually like to see local candidates first, but will entertain interviewing someone willing to pay their own relocation expenses. You may want to consider paying your own moving expenses as an investment in your future with the company. If you believe yourself to be the best candidate, and you know or suspect that your skills are not readily available in the local market, use your experience and skill level as your selling points. As with salary, let the hiring authority bring up the discussion of relocation expenses.

Out of state job seeking is not at all easy or convenient. You could just move and gamble on finding a job when you arrive at your destination, or follow the suggestions I have just outlined and have the advantage of being able to check out an area's employment prospects before committing yourself to a move. You have nothing to lose but the small cost of a few newspapers, directories, phone calls and postage. It's an inexpensive way to research an area.

Notes

Getting Prepared to Promote Yourself: Updating Your Resume

"Attitude and personality are as important as experience and ability. Choose wisely." - Brian Tracy

Your resume(s) and cover letter(s) need to be prepared before scheduling any interviews. Yes, I do mean resumes because you will tailor a resume for each position and customize a cover letter for each company. In the cover letter, indicate why you want to work for this specific company and how you would be considered an asset to their organization. Identify the type of position that you are seeking and list some highlights of your career, as well as your desire to relocate to their area (if applicable). In addition, list some of the information gained from your research of their company. Employers are looking to fill positions, but mainly with people that possess the specific skills and experience in their industry.

You should not send your resume to the personnel department or the hiring manager until after initial contact is made! Be patient. We will address the process of contacting the hiring authorities so that you can introduce yourself and schedule interviews after we have discussed how to update your resumes.

When a professional recruiter performs a review of a resume, he or she immediately considers six key points:

1. In what industry does the applicant have experience?
2. What types of positions has the applicant held?
3. What level of management has the applicant held?
4. What expertise does the candidate bring to the position?
5. Is the candidate open to relocation (if necessary)?
6. What are the salary requirements?

Your resume and cover letter should address all of these areas **with the exception of the salary requirements.** Remember, the employer is interested in making inquiries about your work ethic and past job performance. Therefore, list only business or school references, such as former supervisors, co-workers, professors, or administrators. However, before you begin providing your resume to others and securing interviews, you should personally contact each professional reference and ask for their permission to use them as a reference. Let them know that there is a possibility that they may be contacted for a reference check on your behalf. Also, it is also important that you take the time to periodically update your professional references on how you are doing, as well as your current job status, etc. Your references could become valuable contacts for your employment file.

Another important factor to remember when writing your resume is to eliminate writing generic resumes. Most people make the mistake of writing a generic resume to fill *all* job applications. This is a big no-no if you want your resume to stand out from the hundreds of others received. Generic resumes will not get you noticed and may even work against you. You may have to refine your resume to include catch phrases and experiences outlined in the employer's job description. In other words, your resume should be written to match the employer's needs, not your own. Be truthful. **Do not fabricate any information!** Fabricating information in your resume will often haunt you and possibly lead to your termination. I once placed an executive with a major company as a comptroller. Although doing an excellent job at the time, this executive was asked to resign 90 days after being hired because he had fabricated his education. He did not possess a college degree.

Once you receive an invitation to submit a resume or appear for an interview, you will want your resume to highlight the skills and experiences that make you uniquely qualified for the specific position for which you are applying. I have known top executives who have used at least four different style resumes in their job search. The resumes contain the same basic information, but each one is slanted to highlight a different area of the executive's expertise to catch the eye of the reader. If you do not have the time or experience to make up separate resumes, include an addendum or cover sheet tailored to each specific job opening to describe your related experience.

Another way of making your resume unique is by showing the employer how your background and desires fit within their company's specific needs. In essence, you should include key words that will catch their eye. I really cannot over-emphasize this important point! Make sure that you exhibit a familiarity and suitable level of experience relating with the company's industry, as well as the requirements of the position for which you are applying. Also, keep in mind that your resume is a direct reflection of you. It should be written as a sales pitch. This one document quite literally may or may not get you in the door. The better it is written, the better chance you have to proceed to the next stage. Therefore, it is very important to check for misspelled words or grammatical errors. Looking for employment and getting hired is a daunting challenge itself without shooting yourself in the foot by making these types of errors.

In addition to what has already been mentioned, list your past achievements, cost saving ideas, special training, and anything else that would have a reflection on the quality employee that you are. If you lack the experience requested for a position, then demonstrate your potential and willingness to learn. For example, if you are a recent graduate who does not yet have the work experience, list your academic achievements, leadership abilities, and any other awards or accomplishments received in school or through other community activities. In other words...sell... sell...sell...yourself!

A word to the wise: If you have had several jobs in your career, make sure that you account for all of the time. List the years that you were with each employer, including starting and ending months. If you were attending school or finishing your degree, list this time on your resume. I have had many employers reject resumes of applicants simply based on their time gaps. Unaccounted time raises too many unanswered questions.

When creating your resume, restrict it to one or two pages, three at the most. I have received resumes with up to fifteen pages. Usually, I reject these lengthy resumes outright due to the fact that my corporate clients, those seeking employees, will not take the time to review and to verify all of the information. Most employers will only glance at a resume, and typically for no more than 30 seconds.

They only want to see what is pertinent to their own open position. Therefore, write your resume in a format that is not only eye-catching but also quick and easy to read.

As for the cover letter, it should be addressed directly to the hiring manager's attention. It is important that you have your resume and cover letter with you during the first interview. You should also be prepared to forward your resume and cover letter to the manager prior to the interview (if requested).

If you are unsure about how to create a unique resume that highlights your unique characteristics, you might consider hiring a professional resume writer. Check your local telephone or internet directory to obtain listings for a professional resume writer. Paying an impartial specialist to write your resume would be a smart investment because you want to have a polished, concise document to present to your potential employer.

Notes

Three Steps to
Writing Effective Resumes

With the permission of Linda Matias, President of Career Strides, I would like to highlight her guide on how to construct an effective resume. According to Linda Matias, there are three major techniques that could make the differences between a "strong" resume and an "ok" resume. The three basic techniques can be used not only by the seasoned professional but also by the individual beginning their career search.

These differences include:

1. Format and presentation determine whether the resume is read.

    - The average resume is scanned, not read, for only 8-15 seconds. It either creates a strong impression to the reader immediately or it is set aside. It is similar to the impression that you make on the interviewer. Therefore, make sure that your resume is wearing the equivalent of a "business suit" and not "jeans or flip-flops."

    - Choose a format that compliments your career goal. If you are seeking a job in a field in which you have experience, then use a chronological resume. This type of resume begins with your most recent job and works backward. Conversely, if you are seeking a new type of work, you may want to consider the functional/combination resume. This approach groups your skills together and includes a short chronological work history at the end.

    - Other ways to ensure that your presentation will get noticed include:

        ✓ Use spell check, and also have someone proofread your resume for missing or misused words.

✓ Use a consistent format throughout the resume, i.e. capitalization and punctuation.
✓ Provide quite a bit of white space to accent the strong parts of the resume.
✓ Use no more than 2 fonts.
✓ Laser-print your work on quality white or cream resume parchment paper.

2. Accomplishments tell what you have done. Responsibilities state what you were supposed to have done.

- Not all accomplishments have to be big, but they do need to show that you got results as you carried out your responsibilities. Often, they depict something that you are proud of, or they can simply define what you have done on a daily basis. Many of your routine activities can be quantified and written as accomplishments that demonstrate your experience and knowledge, and provide proof of how you have *helped* the company.

- Here are some things to consider when naming accomplishments (define whenever possible). For instance, did you:

    ✓ save the company money? How much and how?
    ✓ help improve sales? By how much?
    ✓ improve productivity and efficiency?
    ✓ implement any new systems or processes?
    ✓ help launch any new products or services?
    ✓ achieve more with (same or fewer) resources?
    ✓ resolve a major problem with little investment?
    ✓ participate in any technical/operational improvements?
    ✓ exceeded accepted standards for quality or quantity?
    ✓ identify the need for a program or service?
    ✓ prepare any original reports, studies, or documents?

✓ serve on any committees? What was the outcome?

✓ get elected to any boards, teams or task forces?

✓ resolve customer concerns?

✓ get rated as outstanding in performance reviews?

3. Avoid common errors in resume writing.

- Many job seekers either do not know or do not understand the many items that **should not** be present in a resume. Some of these items are listed below along with some recommendations on what to do differently:

    ✓ Instead of using "I", "me", or "my" statements, drop the pronoun and begin the sentence with an action verb. For example, instead of writing, "I wrote the 40-page employee manual", you would write, "Wrote the 40-page employee manual."

    ✓ Simply state your responsibilities and/ or duties rather than using the words, "responsible for" and "duties included."

    ✓ Refrain from including personal information, such as age, health, ethnicity, marriage, and family status. Employers may discard your resume if such information is included because they could someday be accused of hiring bias.

    ✓ Unless you are a model or an actor, you should not include photographs in your resume.

    ✓ Reasons for leaving your previous jobs, or reasons for gaps, should not be included in the resume. For instance, writing "unemployed" is acceptable, but do not state the reason for the unemployment.

    ✓ Extra papers such as letters of recommendation, certificates, or samples of your work clutter your presentation and are also too premature. Therefore, leave them out of the resume and save this for the interview if appropriate.

✓ Salary information should never be included.
✓ Forwarding a list of references is not recommended. Save this piece of information for the interview.

By understanding and utilizing these basic concepts, you will be better prepared to write an effective resume.

The following is a fictitious example of an effective resume:

MARIA HERNANDEZ

598 North Avenue ◆ Lindenhurst, NY 11757
home: 631-555-0861 ◆ cell: 631-555-5961
mhernandez@email.net

SALES & MANAGEMENT
CAREER PROFILE

Seeking to Transfer Broad-Based Skill Set, 15+ Years of Experience in Domestic/Global Markets, and Year-Over-Year Portfolio of Business Development Success into Sales/Management Position

Results-focused, quality-driven professional with extensive experience in business and operational development positions, demonstrating consistent achievement of objectives, strong sales and service skills, and dedication to organizational goals. Advanced presentation and relationship development abilities, with track record of generating multimillion-dollar business growth and engineering red-to-black profit turnarounds.

Core Knowledge & Skill Areas:

- Customer Relationships
- Solutions Selling Strategies
- Import & Export Operations

- Contract Negotiations
- Domestic/Global Sales Growth
- Service Strategies/ Solutions

- Global Business Practices
- Niche Market Development
- Process Redesign/ Streamlining

- Sales Pipeline Expansion
- Team Training & Mentoring
- Regulatory Compliance Issues

CARGO INTERNATIONAL, Long Beach, NY
1994 – Present

INTERNATIONAL OPERATIONS MANAGER (1996 – 2000)
IMPORT MANAGER (1994 – 1996)

Held full responsibility for import and export forwarding operations. Supervised performance of team members, interceded as necessary to resolve problems, and delivered training on improving efficiencies and customer service. Maintained personal rapport and win-win relationships with vendor and clients.
Selected Accomplishments:

- Reversed prior history of under-performing U.S. cargo handling operation by reorganizing processes and implementing new system, turning annual cost of ~**$100,000** into profit of ~**$75,000**.

- Authorized by U.S. Customs to deliver in-bond import leather cargoes to customer designated delivery points, eliminating 1 day on all shipments and allowing customers to improve inventory and production control, with **$1,000+** in per shipment savings.

- Provided specialized delivery service for key customer that affected 6-10 Far East shipments per week and produced **$1,200 to $1,400** per shipment, with deliveries and subsequent profits continuing for 2 consecutive years.

...Professional Experience, Continued...

SEAMAN MARKETING SERVICES, Houston, TX
1987 – 1989

TRADER, INDUSTRIAL CHEMICALS & PLASTICS (1988 – 1989)
SCHEDULER / OPERATIONS SUPERVISOR (1987 – 1988)

Utilized previously established supplier (producer/trader) contacts to support efforts in selling industrial chemicals and plastics into Far East markets for newly-opened Hong Kong office, addressing Pacific Rim demand prior to the construction of regional plants.

Initially recruited to administer all facets of contract supplying Toluene to Coastal States Refining(U.S. Gulf) that brought idled benzene plant on-stream to take advantage of dramatic increase in benzene demand. *Selected Accomplishments:*

◆ Built ongoing business in acetone and industrial alcohols, with preferred freight rates through combination shipping and repeat business (**$40,000** monthly average).

◆ Constructed deal that involved acquisition of raw materials, shipment from Europe to Northeast U.S. through the Lakes to Mid-America (Chicago area), and transfer of resulting P.A. to Taiwan at **$15,000 to $18,000** profit per 1000 metric tons, delivering 6,000 metric tons in 1st year and repeating process in subsequent years.

◆ Met all contract objectives for delivery of 12-20 10,000 bbl. bargeloads of Toluene per week, securing **$12,000** average per bargeload and placing company in preferred position to trade Toluene and Benzene, bringing in additional **$100,000**.

MINEMET, INC., Stamford, CT 1986 – 1987

TRADER, POLYMERS & INDUSTRIAL CHEMICALS

- Purchased plastic resin in bulk in railcars from manufacturers and shipped to packager for repackaging in bags bearing company logo, leading to immediate industry name recognition, volume increases from **30,000 to 60,000** metric tons per year, and average profit gains per 1,000 metric tons from **$8,500 to $11,000.**

- Captured preferred rates from container ocean lines for movements from U.S. to Far East, enabling competition with cargoes of plastics originating in South America.

PROFESSIONAL DEVELOPMENT

PACE UNIVERSITY, New York, NY
120 Credit Hours, BBA in Accounting/Finance/Management Degree Program

Professional Development:
Polymers, Level I – Society of Plastics Industries ◆ Member, International Association of Transportation Agents ◆ Member, North East Chemical Association ◆ Member, South West Chemical Association

Notes

Writing Effective
Cover Letters
By Linda Matias

- As a job seeker, you should not overlook the importance of a cover letter. If written strategically, a cover letter increases your chances of consideration and provides an opportunity to highlight your individuality.

- A cover letter is much more than just a letter stating, "I read the job announcement in Sunday's classified, please accept this letter as an application of interest." It is a statement that tells the reader what they can expect from you if hired.

- The challenging part of writing a cover letter is determining what information to include. After all, the juicy information was included in the resume. What could you possibly add to the cover letter that will add substance to your qualifications?

- Keep in mind that the resume and cover letter have different purposes. A resume demonstrates that you can do the job, it highlights past accomplishments, while a cover letter points out the extent to which you match the job requirement for a specific company and how you fit into that company.

- A well-written cover letter gives you an advantage over your competition because it provides another opportunity to showcase your experience and qualifications.

- The basics of constructing an effective cover letter are as follows:

  ✓ **Sell! Sell! Sell!!**

    - A cover letter is more than just a business letter. It is a sales letter highlighting your

69

value to this specific position. Begin with a strong introduction, layout the benefits you offer, and establish credibility by showcasing your accomplishments.

✓ **Write as you speak.**

- The cover letter should have a professional conversational tone but read as though a real person wrote it. Many people fall into the trap of using big words to communicate their message. Instead, write in a straightforward manner that entices the reader to review the resume comfortably. The words you choose should demonstrate enthusiasm for the position, company, and industry.

✓ **Write from the reader's perspective.**

- Action words should not be reserved for the resume. Begin each sentence with a power word, such as "Accomplished" or "Initiated". Avoid beginning sentences with the word, "I". Like the resume, the focus of the cover letter should be on the hiring company, and beginning too many sentences with "I" puts the spotlight too much on you.

✓ **Avoid a rehash of your resume.**

- Be creative when presenting your qualifications and accomplishments. You do not want to bore the reader by simply repeating the information you included in your resume. Find different ways to communicate the same message. The best way to do this is by selecting three to five major selling points and highlighting them in the body of the cover letter. Doing so will entice the reader to do more than just glance at your resume.

✓ **Ask for an interview.**

- Be proactive. In the last paragraph inform the reader that you will be contacting him or her to setup a possible meeting time. After all, the purpose of applying for a job is to be invited for an interview.

- It is to your benefit to use every tool at your disposal to secure an interview.

- Targeted cover letters add to your portfolio of qualifications and deserve as much consideration as a resume.

The following is a fictitious example of an effective cover letter:

MARIA HERNANDEZ
598 North Avenue ◆ Lindenhurst, NY 11757
home: 631-555-0861 ◆ cell: 631-555-5961
mhernandez@email.net

<Date>

<Name of Hiring Manager, Title>
<Name of Company>
<Address>
<City, State Zip>

Dear <Mr. or Ms.><Last Name>:

It was with great interest that I learned about your opening for a Sales-Service Representative for ABC Pharmaceutical Services. On your corporate web site, I noted that a key selling point for ABC is its strong commitment to customer service and value: "Our customers enjoy an absolutely unequaled level of service, value, convenience and effortless pharmacy involvement." Throughout my career, I have emphasized this same level of dedication to sales and service; thus, I feel that my skills and your organization's current goals are an ideal match.

Please allow me to reference some highlights from my career that may be of interest to you:

- With Seaman Marketing Services, I leveraged supplier relationships to build our acetone and industrial alcohol business within the Far East market, leading to 5-figure profit gains and enhanced positioning;
- With Widget Inc., I established a sales niche for industrial chemicals and plastics that brought in an average of $10,000 to $20,000 per week;
- With Cargo International, I improved our customer service significantly by petitioning U.S. Customs to re-route specific deliveries to customer-designated locations, saving them approximately $1,000 in shipment costs.

In these examples, as well as throughout my career, I have met and exceeded expectations in sales and service objectives through an uncompromising focus on customer needs and relationship building. Now, I would like to do the same for your organization.

My résumé will provide additional details regarding my background and accomplishments. I would welcome the opportunity for a personal interview to discuss the results you can expect from me.

Thank you for your time and consideration.

Sincerely,

Maria Hernandez

Enclosure   Courtesy of CareerStrides

Notes

Making Contact and Promoting Yourself

**"Think before you act, and then act decisively.
Fortune favors the brave." Brian Tracy**

Now that your resume and cover letter are completed, you can begin using your networking file and start calling potential employers. Call the manager or hiring authority referred to you by one of your contacts and if he/she is not available do not leave a voice mail message. If someone other than the hiring authority answers your call, be professional, yet persistent, until you make direct contact with that person. Once you have made direct contact, introduce yourself in a friendly, polite manner. Right away, mention the name of the contact person who suggested you call. Your initial conversation might go like this: "Hello, Mr. Yung, this is Austin VanDeKerkhove. Denise Grothe suggested that I call you." Relax! You have initiated the conversation!

Acknowledge that you were referred to them with the possibility that he/she might have a job opening in the department or perhaps a colleague in the company has an employment need. This is not the time to be timid. You never have another chance to make a first impression. Therefore, give it your all but attempt to keep your conversation brief and direct rather than long-winded. Show your familiarity with the company and their products or services from the beginning. Remember, you put a lot of research into each company so utilize it. Discuss your skills and experience. Conclude the conversation by asking when you can schedule an interview. Be prepared to forward your cover letter and resume to this person prior to any interview.

If you discover that this contact does not have any job openings, ask them if they know someone who may be hiring. This contact may be comfortable referring you to a colleague at another company because you have mentioned the person who referred you, as well as showed them

75

your professional attitude and familiarity with the industry. You may need to go through this process over and over again. Follow this same process for each person that you contact, but ask the previous contact if you may use his/her name as a referral to the new company. Within a short period of time you could conceivably have over one hundred contact names in your networking file!

People will always talk to a referral from a friend or personal acquaintance. Therefore, do not be reluctant to make calls to those individuals, and always thank them for their assistance. Contacting these types of referrals and remembering your manners (like saying, "thank-you") is often crucial to a job search. When you do find a job opening, you have just eliminated a great deal of your competition by finding out about the position first and introducing yourself to the manager or hiring agent with a referral from someone he/she knows.

Be prepared that your first few calls may not be successful. However, do not lose faith in this process because eventually you *will* succeed. You have to remember that you are learning a new skill and you will improve with each phone call. Consider your first calls as "practice" calls. Review your technique after each call and make any necessary improvements to your presentation. Your success in this process can be measured by whether or not you secure a job interview or gain new contact names. At the end of this process, note which companies you have contacted, identify the person with whom you spoke, explain the outcome, and place this information in your networking file.

Notes

Overcoming Obstacles
as You Make Contact

"Difficulties come not to obstruct, but to instruct." Brian Tracy

With today's high-tech communication systems, it sometimes seems next to impossible to speak with a live voice when calling companies, but getting an actual person on the phone should not be impossible if you learn a few tricks of the trade.

Make your calls at or before 8:30 a.m. or after 5:00 p.m. when the person you are trying to reach would more likely be at his or her desk. If you are routed to an automated "after hours" message, dial the persons extension. The call should go straight through to their desk. If you are connected into the person's voice mail attempt to contact them at a different time of day or dial the next extension in sequence.

Most departments have sequential phone numbers. When you reach a live person, ask for help. Explain who you are and who you are trying to reach. If the individual that you are attempting to contact is not available, ask if the person with whom you are speaking is in a position close to your contact. If so, ask when your contact might return or when would be the best time to reach them. Ask the person that you are speaking with if they would leave a written message and remember to mention who referred you and why you are calling.

If the company phone system allows you to dial the operator or receptionist, then do so. This option removes you from the technology loop and gives you an opportunity to talk to a live voice. Ask the operator or receptionist if the person you are trying to contact is in the building. If not available, ask what would be the best time to reach them. Politely decline the offer to be put through to your contact's voice mail. Instead, request that the operator or receptionist please deliver a written message. When stating your message, make sure that you are clear in the purpose of your call. Indicate who you are, why you are calling, and identify the name of the person who referred you. State the information slowly and repeat your callback number at least twice. It is also a good idea to spell out both your name and the name of the person who referred you, especially if the names are not particularly familiar.

E-mails are a popular method of quick communication but may not be the right tool when looking for a job. E-mail communications are *very* informal and impersonal. I typically receive close to eighty e-mails a day and really cannot take the time to read them all. Therefore, if you do not want to have your e-mail deleted along with all the other unsolicited e-mails then the best way to utilize email is to get out of email. In other words, when attempting to communicate with an employer, suggest a personal meeting or a phone call as the next step. Selling oneself is much easier on a one-on-one basis rather than trying to accomplish this with an impersonal approach. Use your researching skills to find phone numbers and extensions for your contacts. Let the person you are trying to call hear your voice. If you believe that you have identified a good job opportunity, look for ways to develop a personal touch during this selection process. Sending a personal note is much better than sending an e-mail. Phone calls will create the opportunity to build a rapport with the hiring authority. During a telephone conversation, you will be given the opportunity to answer any concerning your experiences, abilities, desires, and character.

Again, remember, that you are rarely given a second chance to make a first impression. Therefore, make a great impression during your telephone conversation so that you will more likely be asked to interview and meet with the hiring authority. After all, face-to-face conversation is the ultimate way to communicate when trying to obtain a position.

Notes

Fear of Rejection

"Success is the ability to go from failure to failure without losing your enthusiasm." Sir Winston Churchill

Making telephone calls to market yourself has never been an easy task As a recruiter, it took me a long time to become comfortable in making these necessary contacts with others. My reluctance in calling was influenced by my fear of rejection. However, I quickly began to understand that it was a necessary part of my business and a must for you in your job search.

This is a time where you will rely primarily on your self-discipline and your self-discipline will guide you in this process. We all have a tendency to put off what we do not like doing. When I first entered the field of recruiting, my biggest challenge was picking up the phone and contacting prospective companies. I share this with you not to make you more anxious but to emphasize the importance of making these spontaneous calls (also known as cold calls) to prospective companies or employers. In preparing for these types of calls, I have provided a few suggestions to help you overcome those anxieties and become more comfortable and successful in making them.

1. Prepare a short script for yourself and practice delivering it. Keep in mind that you will not recite it, but use it as a reference. Your speech should flow naturally and not sound like a canned presentation. Another important factor to think about is *when* you will say the things that you have planned.

2. Prior to making your calls, create an active list of all of the companies that you have researched and are going to contact. You will find it beneficial to complete this list in the evening before you make the calls.

3. Force yourself into making that first call and you will discover that subsequent calls will become easier. In other words, you will start developing more confidence in yourself and in what you are doing through each call you make.

4. Begin your calling early in the day. Most managers are in their offices first thing in the morning or late in the day. Avoid making these calls during mid mornings and mid afternoons as these are typically not the best times to reach the individuals that you are attempting to contact.

5. Once again, attitude is most important. Be enthusiastic and positive. This usually does not happen without practice. Therefore, practice your script and be comfortable delivering it. Use a friend or relative as an audience and request their constructive analysis.

6. Be flexible and prepared to answer any questions.

7. Finally, make sure that you ask for referrals.

Notes

Telephone Calling Guide

If you have previously sent the hiring manager a letter, begin the conversation by making reference to that document. Gain immediate rapport by asking questions that will engage his/her attention. Asking questions that simply require a **"yes"** or **"no"** answer will usually get you a "no" response. Whatever you do, refrain from beginning the conversation by asking whether or not the company is hiring.

You might consider beginning the conversation with the following: "Hello, my name is John Doe, Ann Bishop suggested that I call you as someone who could give me some advice. I have been working as a plant accountant for the past seven years and my main responsibilities have included job costing, as well as being a labor and material analyst. Since I am heavily involved with my position, I would like to talk with someone who could give me a broader overview of the market for my specialty in this area." After providing this individual with this brief introduction, you should have his or her attention and may now begin to ask the following (or similar) questions:

- Would you say that my specialty and experience is in demand in this market?
- What do you see as long-term expectations in this field?
- Which companies that you are familiar with may be expanding their work force?
- What companies, which you are familiar with, have been recently awarded new contracts?
- Who would be interested in someone with my experience and education?
- Could you identify any companies that may be considering hiring at this time?

Keep in mind that you are learning valuable information from this individual, so let him/her do the talking. If not, you will probably discover that the information that you did learn will be limited by the amount of speaking attributed by you. This is the prime opportunity to get to know the decision maker a little more and to develop a rapport with him/her. You might even feel comfortable in calling this person back from time to time for additional advice.

When concluding your call always ask the following question, "Given my experience, education, qualifications, etc., do you know of any company or person that I could contact to enhance my career?" If given a name, ask if they know of any additional contacts, and also if you can use their name as a referral. This is an excellent way to build your referral list and to open your conversation with the name of who referred you.

Consider job hunting as a numbers game. The more people you talk with the sooner you will find employment. If by chance the individual that you talk with has an immediate opening, do not just say "thank you" and that you will "follow up" thus ending the conversation. Instead, reply like you are ready to go to work. Say something like, "This is great. I could stop by tomorrow. Is there a time that would be convenient for you?" If asked to send a resume, state that you had planned to be on their side of town and request if you could just drop it off. If this company does not have an opening at this time respond with something like, "Mr. Jones, I would like to leave my name and phone number just in case you think of someone who might be able to help me." **Always** follow up each conversation with a thank you letter thanking them for their time spent with you.

Notes

Planning and
Scheduling Your Day

Job-hunting often appears grueling because many people do not assume the responsibility of organizing and planning their day. Accomplishing a task like this takes discipline and motivation on their part. Without a preconceived plan including a working schedule, they will be wasting valuable time and effort figuring out what they are going to do with their day. As the saying goes, "time is money." Therefore, spend it wisely because if you waste too much valuable time by not being productive, you like many other people, will fail to land a job quickly.

Work on your plan ahead of time, (perhaps the previous evening) by listing the companies you are going to call, the contact names and telephone numbers, who referred you, and a working schedule of the times that you plan on contacting these individuals. Keep in mind that most employers are in their offices early or stay late. The bulk of your employer calls should be accomplished in the mornings before 9:00 am. or in the afternoon after 4:30 pm. If you do this, I assure you that your day will start early, be more effective, and hopefully produce the results that you are trying to accomplish. Make sure you have made up your introduction script and practice using it. Keep it handy when making your calls to potential employers. *Do not attempt to wing it.* The key to the call is information gathering, asking questions, knowing what you are going to say and how you are going to say it, and also getting additional referrals. Be creative and innovative. Your script must be written as a piece of sales copy. You are selling yourself to the employer.

Next, it is *vital* that you continue to expand on your referrals list. This list should be referred to as the "Who do you know" list because you are continuing to ask people "Who do you know?" Get in touch with any newly acquired individuals that have been referred to you from previous contacts after your morning employers calls. After spending some time with them, either go to the web or use the different guides discussed in the **Networking** chapter to do your research on companies you are interested in.

Keep focused, job- hunting is not for the faint at heart. If you fail to plan then expect to fail. If you cannot seem to organize your day then you have just not properly planned your day. There are many good quality jobs are out there, you just have to work harder and smarter than the next guy to find them. If you are to be successful you must plan and schedule your day as a successful person does. It's all up to you. You are the maker of your own environment.

Notes

What Employers
Look For

"Whenever you are asked if you can do a job, tell 'em 'Certainly I can!' Then get busy and find out how to do it." – Theodore Roosevelt

Far too many times a candidate will focus on the "what's in it for me" attitude when searching for a job. These "what's in it for me" items include salary, benefits, responsibilities, title, location and industry. On the other side of the fence, employers have a different set of standards on what they are looking for and expecting from a candidate. The sooner you understand this difference the better off you will be in developing a successful job search.

What employers look for is **your ability to do the job.** When I, as a recruiter, post a job or place an ad, I typically expect about 20% of the responders to be qualified to perform at least the basic functions as outlined in the ad. These individuals deserve closer scrutiny. The remainder have either read themselves into the ad or they are just hoping that the employer will have other needs that they would be qualified for. At times I have to question just how many of these individuals have really looked at the job description. The point that I am attempting to illustrate is to *not* waste your time responding to ads posted if you are not qualified to perform at least the basic tasks as outlined in the job description. In responding to an ad, I have advised you to edit your resume to include key words as indicated in the ad. Do this also when writing up your cover letter. Emphasize your skill levels and work experience directly relating to what the employer is looking for.

What employers look for is **leadership.** Even if you have not performed in a defined leadership role, employers look for areas of your experience where you have contributed ideas for cost savings, new methods for improved job productivity, or set superior work examples to your peers. Show managers that you have the initiative to assume a leadership role regardless of what level you work.

What employers look for is **attitude.** To me, and a great number of other people, attitude is everything. If an employer has a candidate who possesses a great desire to be the best that they can be, has a high energy level, and is full of enthusiasm, he knows that it will encourage others to reach towards a higher standard. A positive attitude has a tendency to motivate others, and creates in them a desire to achieve higher levels of productivity. Show each employer a high level of enthusiasm for their business and you will certainly increase your chances of receiving an offer. Simply put, act as though you have a strong desire to profit their business.

What employers look for is **self-confidence.** Confidence is a trait of a successful individual. Employers look for candidates who show an air of confidence. Individuals who will look them in the eye and show in their speech, mannerism, posture, and body language that they can be trusted to perform and produce the desired results. Individuals who are result- oriented with a successful track record should look the part, be the part and act the part. Show your ongoing record of accomplishments and successes.

What employers look for is **communication skills.** Proper communication is a necessity in today's business world. Good communicators possess outstanding written and oral skills and use them effectively. They demonstrate the ability to communicate their ideals and beliefs to superiors, peers, and subordinates to achieve their own, and the company's objectives and goals.

A recent survey was conducted asking Hiring Authorities and Executive Recruiters as to what characteristics were valued most in prospective candidates. Included were:

- Personality 44%
- Skills/Knowledge 28%
- Creativity/Intelligence 28%

Notes

The First Interview

"Ask for what you want. Ask for help, ask for input, ask for advice and ideals—but never be afraid to ask." - Brian Tracy

If you have gotten this far in the process, it is because you handled yourself well during your initial contact with the hiring authority. What you do from this point on will determine whether or not you get the job.

One of the biggest complaints that I hear from employers is that the majority of job candidates lack any information on the company with whom they are interviewing. Therefore, I would advise that you equip yourself to be able to answer questions concerning the company and the position during the interview. Also, be prepared to ask pertinent, relevant questions to demonstrate that you are genuinely interested in the company and the position. Again, avoid asking about salary, vacation time, or benefits. Let the employer bring up these subjects and make the offer. Keep your answers short and focused, and only say what the interviewer wants to hear.

After making the effort of introducing yourself to the department chair and securing the interview, you will want to be certain that you create the best first impression. Although some of this interview advice may seem obvious, take the time to familiarize yourself with these key points. A careless mistake could cost you the opportunity of being offered the job. The better prepared you are, the more advantage you will have over the other candidates applying for the position.

Interview DON'TS:

- Never arrive late for an interview. In fact, arrive at least fifteen to twenty minutes early. While waiting in the lobby or reception area, exude an air of poise and confidence. Do not fidget or appear impatient. The front office staff will routinely share their first impression of you with the management.

- Eating, drinking, or chewing gum during a conversation is often considered rude, unprofessional, and should not be done during an interview. If offered, politely decline until after the interview concludes. Chewing on breath mints is also not acceptable. Finish them before or while waiting for your appointment.

- Under no circumstances should you take a phone call during an interview. If you must bring your cell phone in with you, be certain that it is turned OFF! I well remember attempting to interview a young woman for an administrative position that I had open in my own office. Although she had the necessary qualifications for the position, I had to terminate our meeting because she answered her cell phone several times during the first fifteen minutes of the interview. Of course, she was not offered the job.

- Nose rings, tongue rings, eyebrow rings, or anything else that may distract the person interviewing you should not be worn. Prove that you are a professional person and qualified for the position by presenting a well-groomed appearance. I once had an employer call me after he had conducted an interview with a qualified candidate that I had sent him for a receptionist position. He had difficulty understanding her speech. She explained that she could not speak very well because over the weekend she had a spike put through her tongue, and would take some time getting used to. Considering the position that she was interviewing for was to speak to others, she did not get the job.

- Avoid being "long winded" in your conversation. Answer any questions asked directly and briefly. I'll never forget an interview I conducted with a man who would not stop talking. He talked himself into and out of a job in one meeting. I was afraid to ask him any more questions for fear of having to spend the rest of the day with him!

- Under no circumstance should you criticize or condemn your previous employer, even if you feel that it is justifiable to do so. It is an industry rule not to disparage your former manager. Remember, you are learning just how important networking can

94

be. Be discreet, your former boss might know people who know the people that are conducting the interview.

- Salary, vacations, 401ks, and other benefits are important topics, but not during the interview. If the employer is interested in the topic allow him or her the opportunity to bring it up. Your job is to *sell yourself* to the employer so that the job offer will be made.

Interview DO'S

- Go to bed early the night before the interview so that you may be fully rested.

- Know the best business attire to wear for an interview. Dress moderately to reflect a good image. Consider the applied position and then dress appropriately for that type of position. It may not be to your benefit to wear a three- piece suit if you are applying for a construction management position nor would you wear jeans and a polo shirt for an administrative position. Keep jewelry to a tasteful minimum. As you already have heard throughout this book, first impressions are very important.

- Always sell your ability and desire to do the job. This is the most important aspect of the interview. Review the information that you have gained in your research and prepare a list of intelligent and engaging questions that you will want to ask about the company and the position. Your initiative will greatly impress the interviewer. He or she will know that you have done your homework. If you really want to get the interviewer's attention ask these two questions:

  ✓ What do you see as the greatest challenge for this position?
  ✓ What are the most important qualities you are looking for in a candidate for this particular position?

Once you have asked these two questions, listen attentively to the answers and be prepared to highlight your experience and talents that meet the challenges and fulfill the qualities the interviewer mentioned.

- Be alert and look alert. Remember that the key to interviewing is listening attentively to the interviewer and answering questions honestly and succinctly.

  - ✓ Also, show that you have good listening skills. Making and maintaining eye contact with the interviewer displays effective communication. Hence, you should look at the interviewer and not out the window. Slouching in your seat is unacceptable, as is fidgeting, playing with your hair, biting your nails, or any other distracting behaviors.

- Adjust the tone of your voice and the speed of your speech to match that of the interviewer. For example, if the interviewer speaks slowly then slow down your speech. However, if he/she is speaking quickly, then pick up your pace.

- Leave the salary open, even when filling out the job application. If the employer asks you what you are willing to accept as salary, respond by stating that you are confident that if an offer is extended, it will be fair. Stress that you are most interested in the overall opportunity that comes with joining the company and fulfilling the position. Whatever you do, avoid committing yourself to a salary level because you may find that what you would accept may be lower than what the employer was planning to offer you. Thus, you have cheated yourself out of the better income. Instead, let the employer commit to a salary level, and once this offer has been extended, you can negotiate for a better deal if necessary. You should not be surprised to find that the offer may be less than what you expect, or less than what you know you are worth because the job market can be very, very restrictive. In cases such as this, you need to ask yourself, "Would you rather have a good job paying less money than you would like to receive at the start, or would you rather have no job at all?" Although this job may not pay what you expected, it may give you the experience you need before obtaining a more lucrative job.

- On at least two occasions during the interview, ask for the job. You are never going to get hired unless you ask for the job, or at the very least let the interviewer know that you are genuinely interested in the position. I have had many clients tell me that the candidates looked good and seemed qualified, but that the level of interest was unclear because the candidate never asked to be hired for the position. Make them aware that not only are you qualified, but *want* the opportunity. Believe me; it is tough to turn down someone who asks for the job. Not taking this chance could be read by the interviewer as being uncommitted to this position. Be forward, boldly ask one or more of these three questions:

- ✓ Do you have any objections that would prevent you from making an offer now?
- ✓ When would you like me to start?
- ✓ What critical task would you have me doing first?

Asking for the job on the first interview may seem a little forward, but this is how it is done in the corporate world. You should find yourself invited back more often.

- Upon the conclusion of the interview, it is imperative for you to make a closing statement (especially if you want a second interview). Ask these three questions:

- ✓ Is there any reason you would not consider inviting me back for a second interview?
- ✓ When would you like to schedule our next meeting?
- ✓ Who will I meet in the second interview?

Most people assume that their past work experience is the deciding factor in getting hired. While skills and experiences are always important, your communication ability can be the ultimate decision maker on your getting hired or not. There have been times when a lesser-experienced individual was hired over someone with more experience simply due to his or her excellent communication skills. This is why it is important to prepare yourself before the first interview. Not only do you want to be able to answer any questions posed to you, but also you want to be able to ask intelligent questions and really listen to and understand the interviewer's answers. Asking questions does not make you look foolish, as *good* communicators will ask many intelligent questions.

Making other people feel important and special is crucial to successful communications. Be certain that your attention is focused on the person with whom you are speaking. Taking steps to improve one's communication skills is viably important and will offer many long-term rewards in your career.

If you do not receive a job offer after your first interview, or even after your second, do not become discouraged. We in the recruiting field expect a 1 to 5 ratio, that is one job offer for every five interviews arranged, and we are the professionals who prepare the candidates and brief the employers prior to the interview. You should expect a job offer after interviewing with an average of five companies, but this is not to imply that you will not be hired on your first. Each completed interview takes you closer to your goal of getting the job.

Notes

Top Interview Questions

The results of a survey of over 2,000 corporate recruiters and hiring managers provide the fifteen most frequently asked interview questions. Rather than being caught off guard, prepare yourself with a complete but brief response to each of the following questions.

- ✓ Describe your ideal job and/or boss.
- ✓ Why are you looking for a job? Why are you leaving your current position?
- ✓ What unique experiences or qualifications separate you from other candidates?
- ✓ Tell me about yourself.
- ✓ What are your strengths and weaknesses?
- ✓ Describe some of your short-term and long-term goals.
- ✓ Describe a time when you were faced with a challenging (work) situation and explain the outcome after you handled it.
- ✓ What are your salary requirements?
- ✓ Why are you interested in this position or this company?
- ✓ What would your former manager and colleagues say about you?
- ✓ What were the best and worst aspects of your previous jobs?
- ✓ What do you know about our company?
- ✓ What motivates you? How do you motivate others?
- ✓ Are you willing to relocate?

Notes

Tell Me About Yourself

This is perhaps the most frequently asked question during an interview. Even though most candidates expect this question, they find it the most difficult to answer. The key to answering this question successfully is by offering a response that supports your career objective(s). This means you should not respond with anything related to hobbies, spouse, or extra-curricular activities.

Keep in mind that the interview process is used as a method to either eliminate or advance you as a potential candidate. Questions asked are normally intended to determine your skill level, experience, personality, and how you stack up against the other candidates being considered for the position. The interviewer also takes into consideration just how well you match with the company. He/she is attempting to determine if what you offer will meet with the company's goals and objectives.

Therefore, the question, "tell me about yourself" must be answered with care and thought on your part. Begin by providing a brief introduction about yourself and interject attributes that are key to the open position. Next, provide a recent work history of yourself that supports your job objective. In addition, connect your work history with the needs of the hiring company. In other words, make sure that the interviewer understands how your experiences are transferable to the position that you are seeking. Finally, ask questions. By asking questions you are gaining partial control of the interview. However, do not ask a question just for the sake of asking. The questions you ask should give you further insight as to the job responsibilities and skill levels required for the position.

Notes

Profile Questions

The following questions are for you as a candidate to review and come up with   your own answers. I have used these as a part of my interviewing process in evaluating specific candidates for management positions, so please take your time in answering. The reason for this exercise is to get you thinking about your pervious job experiences and your approach in handling different situations. I have always felt that the more you prepare yourself for the interview the better off you will be. One or two, if not all, may be asked by the interviewer during your first or second interview.

- How do your managers, peers and subordinates perceive you collectively and separately?

- What type of role did you play on a team? What role do you prefer to play?

- Take me through a time when you took a product or idea from inception to fruition.

- Describe how you work under tight deadlines. How is that different from other times?

- What tools or resources have enhanced your effectiveness or efficiency in your work place?

- What characteristics do you exhibit to show that you have a good work ethic?

- How have you improved communication within your group?

- In the last few years, in what part of your professional skill set have you improved the most? How do you know you have made improvements?

- What is your definition of working too hard? How do you manage stress?

- How did you create opportunity for yourself in your previous company?

- What are the most important characteristics in a job that you are looking for, and why?

- If you were a new person on a team, what things would you do to gain the respect and positioning within the group?

Notes

Prepare for Unusual
and Outlandish Questions

You may have thought that we have addressed nearly all of the questions that you could expect to be asked during your interviewing sessions. Well, perhaps we have not addressed quite *all* of them. Some people just never seem to quit thinking up new, unusual, and outlandish questions to ask candidates during an already stressful interview.

A recent article that was prepared and developed by **Office Team,** a staffing service specializing in highly skilled professionals appeared in the California Job Journal. It was revealed that when 150 executives from the Nations 1000 largest companies were asked for the strangest questions asked by hiring managers during an interview, the responses ranged from the unusual to the outrageous as indicated by the following questions:

- "What is your favorite color?"
- "If you could be any animal, what animal would it be?"
- "If you were having a dinner party and could invite three famous people, who would they be?"
- "What is the last book that you read?"

Actually, the interviewer is interested in the "why" behind the applicant's answer because it often sheds light on his or her personality. The reason given for citing a particular book or dinner guest, for instance, could prompt conversation that a resume or a skills–based interview question alone would not.

Other questions that may reveal a job candidate's aspirations might include:

- "What did you want to be when you were 10 years old?"
- "What were your favorite classes in high school?"
- v "Do you see yourself in my position in the future?"

With these questions, hiring managers seek to understand the applicant's goals and ambitions over time. The hiring manager is also attempting to discover how quickly the candidate expects to advance in the organization and the importance he or she assigns to rank and title.

This last set of unusual questions that executives were asked seems to defy classification:

- "Why are manholes covers round?"
- "What would I find in your refrigerator?"
- "How would taking this job change your life?"
- "What made you move to a backward city like this one?"

Asking a truly unexpected question will likely elicit a candid, unrehearsed response, and as a bonus, the hiring manager will get a better sense of the person's sense of humor and ability to think quickly.

The article further indicates several valuable tips for preparing yourself for these types of questions:

- Do some homework ahead of time.
- Ask the people in your network about the strangest questions that they were asked in an interview, how they responded to them, and what (if anything) they would have done differently.
- The point is not to prepare for every question, but to practice thinking on your feet.

Ask for clarification. If you do not understand a question, rephrase it by saying, "Do you mean..." or ask for more detail. This will put you on the same page as the interviewer and enable you to provide a targeted response.

Feeling stress during an interview is to be expected. Excessive stress, however, could cause you to "ramble" or give only "yes" or "no" answers. Do not allow nervousness to get the best of you. If you need a moment to think about how to answer a question, ask for it, or stall for time by making a comment about the question, such as "that's a great question" or "what an intriguing question."

You may find yourself meeting with several interviewers at a particular company, some less prepared and experienced than others. Do not assume the worst. Be patient with each successive meeting, even when the same questions are being asked multiple times. Your calm demeanor will count in your favor in the final selection.

Finally, if it turns out that you need more preparation, have a friend run you through a practice interview, or consider one of the helpful interview books on the market. Most of these books list hundreds of typical questions and potential answers, along with additional advice on how to handle the unusual and unexpected ones.

By the way, just in case you were wondering, I believe manhole covers are round to prevent them from falling in.

Notes

Questions That Need Answering

There are specific questions that you need to be concerned about when interviewing with a potential employer. You may or may not have considered all of them, so I have listed what I feel are important issues you should find out about before *accepting* an offer.

- Salary/income progression-short and long term, bonuses-how earned, profit sharing, stock options, predicted public offering? (If privately held)

- Benefits-What are they and when is eligibility? Who pays?

- Job description-What do I do for my salary? What are the expectations?

- Opportunities for growth-how soon, what determines personal growth opportunities? Is company growth projected as well?

- How does the company rate within the industry, previous/projected sales figures, market share? What is company's track record? Have they restructured, made acquisitions, recently been acquired?

- Any work quotas involved?

- What exactly is the work environment like?

- What is the company's history?

- Any new product developments, current with new technologies, what challenges for me?

- What is the turnover rate? Is this a new position?

Notes

Look and Act the Part

I cannot tell you how many times an employer has surprised me with whom they have chosen to hire when I thought that the individual would not have been my top choice. In asking why, they normally respond by saying, "Well, he/she did not have the experience and skill level as the other candidates, but we liked him/her so well that we just felt he/she would be trainable and fit into our team environment." This goes to show that experience does not always count as the deciding factor in being hired.

What does count if not experience? The principal reasons that people are initially considered for jobs are appearance, first impressions of speaking ability, and body language. Again, it is vital that you dress appropriately or you will not get past the initial interview.

Frequently, an employer will make a decision on seriously considering the candidate for hire either immediately or right after the candidate sits down. This information reinforces the importance of a well-groomed appearance and a confident manner. **First impressions mean almost everything!**

I will give you an example of what happened to one of my candidates on a second interview conducted by the CEO of a major corporation. This candidate was being considered for a Corporate Engineering Manager's position and during his first interview everyone who met with him was very impressed by his expertise and management credentials. They were convinced that this meeting would be a sure thing resulting in him being hired. To their amazement he spent merely minutes with the CEO and was ushered out the door. What could have possibly gone wrong? After about an hour, the Director of Human Relations called and informed me about the candidate's appearance. Unfortunately, the candidate wore an outdated business suit that appeared not to have been pressed, and his tie did not match. Why this candidate did not prepare himself properly for the second interview, especially when being conducted by the president,

I will never know. When the candidate finally called sounding very disappointed, I asked him why he did not wear the same suit that he wore on the first interview? He replied that he had only two suits and *that* suit was in the cleaners. The president was looking for an image, and the one provided by the candidate was not the one that he wanted representing his company at that level of position. First impressions count immensely.

What to wear: Men

Based on the above disaster, make sure that your suit is conservative in appearance, up to date, cleaned, and pressed. I always advise my candidates to wear a business suit or a sports coat with matching slacks if they are interviewing for an executive level position. Of course, this will depend on your locale or trade. I have always had the opinion that being overdressed was better than being underdressed for an interview. Wear a long-sleeve white or pale blue shirt and a coordinated silk tie. No bow ties, unless you are interviewing as a physicist. Make sure that your shoes are polished. Avoid heavy cologne. Have a fresh haircut; men who wear short hairstyles seem to fair better in most interviews. Making a good first impression should be paramount in conducting your job search.

What to wear: Women

Here is another story that I would like to share with you. I was interviewing a young woman for an administrative position and was in the process of setting up a meeting for her with one of my clients for an early morning interview. I made a big mistake by just telling her to dress nicely and to look her best, and neglected to tell her to wear proper business attire. The employer called me after the interview and asked what type of job this young lady was interviewing for. It seemed that she had arrived wearing a low cut cocktail dress, high heel shoes with straps that tie up to mid calf, net stockings, and long earrings. She did make quite an impression, but unfortunately, the wrong one.

Professional or white-collar women have an abundance of choices on what to wear. Therefore, increasing the chance for mistakes. Always wear a suit, skirt, or dress *with a jacket.* Your outfit should be on the conservative side unless you are in the fashion field or

114

live in a casual area. Avoid taking your purse with you during the interview. Instead, carry a briefcase or a satchel type case. Wearing a jacket and carrying a briefcase gives the impression that you have clout. Check your personal appearance. Jewelry should be worn where appropriate and kept to a minimum. Hair should be clean and neat, fingernails manicured, and minimal make-up applied. Short skirts may be in fashion, but do not wear one for the first interview. It is best to observe what the other women are wearing and then modify your wardrobe for the second interview if you would like.

Body language: for all

Crossing your arms is one of the most negative signs of body language and should *never* be done during the interview. Statistics have shown that only 15% of getting hired was based primarily on qualifications. It is more about how you handle yourself during the interview. Become sensitive to your tone of voice, posture, facial expressions, attitude, and eye contact (all of which give signs about your feelings and attitudes). After becoming sensitive to these traits in yourself, face the interview in a relaxed and open manner.

- Smile. I like being around people who know how to smile, and so does an employer.

- Maintain good eye contact. It shows that you are attentive.

- Speak in a firm, confident voice. Develop rapport with small talk before addressing the important issues.

- Give a good firm handshake. A handshake tells a lot about the individual.

  I personally do not like receiving a weak handshake. It gives me the impression that either they are not particularly interested in meeting me or they lack self-confidence.

- Ask if you could take notes during the interview. Your portfolio should have these body language guides written down as a reminder.

- Maintain a good posture. Mirror the interviewer's physical posture and maintain a simple, straight posture to give the appearance of balance, openness, and sincerity.

I am aware that some of this text is covered throughout the book and principally in the First Interview section. But knowing the importance of how well you present and conduct yourself during the interview may just determine whether you get the job or not.

Notes

The Second Interview

Most companies require a second interview that must also be prepared for, and believe me, the second interview is just as important as the first. Interviewers who meet with you for the second time will view you in a different perspective as they become more comfortable with you. They will expect that you will be more informed about their company and express an even greater enthusiasm for the career opportunity being extended to you. Understand that this is all part of the process of getting hired.

During the second interview you will likely be meeting new interviewers and they will typically conduct the interview similar to the first interview. In the interviewer's eyes, you have successfully passed the first reviewing stage. Therefore, you must be qualified and a strong candidate for their position. However, they will still need some convincing as to your abilities, experiences, and personal desires. I have seen too many people blow their second interview because they let their guard down and conducted this phase as if it were just a formality. On the contrary, you should be as sharp and alert as you were during your first interview. Keep in mind that the people you will meet during the second interview are most likely the final decision makers in the hiring process.

After having gone through the first interview, you will be better informed concerning the company and the job responsibilities of the position. Therefore, you should be better prepared to answer and ask specific questions concerning your role in the organization. Prepare yourself for this second meeting by making up a list of questions that you want answered and explain your relative experiences as they relate to the employers needs. Once again, you will need to continue selling your ability and desire to do the job and to join their company. If you follow the guidelines as outlined for your first interview the second should not propose a reason for undue concern.

Just a reminder, when waiting in the reception area do not pace the floor or keep looking at your watch if the interview is late getting started. Instead, relax, smile, and appear comfortable. Be polite to the receptionists and front office staff. Believe it or not, it is not uncommon for employers to have their receptionists observe the behavior of candidates as they wait for interviews. These employers want to know about first impressions you made, and the receptionist's opinion on how you conducted yourself during the time spent in their areas. Be on your toes at all times and you should do well. Again, before leaving the second interview, make sure that you ask for the job.

Notes

Communication
for Career Success

A characteristic of a successful person is the ability to master the art of communication to oneself and the ability to master the art of communication to others. – Anthony Robbins

Career and life success very much depends upon our ability to communicate effectively to others and how well we think successfully or communicate to ourselves. Communicating effectively to others facilitates support, understanding, respect, cooperation, and achievement. Communicating effectively to ourselves facilitates motivation, self respect, confidence, and achievement. Whether you are sitting for an interview, talking to your teammates on the job, or presenting your ideas to your supervisors, effective communication will pave the way to your success.

Purpose, Poise, And Passion

Imagine or think of someone you recognize as a role model, someone you admire for their character, their success in their careers, the respect that person receives from others, and the respect that person communicates to others. What are the traits or qualities of that individual that you would like to duplicate? Very likely, along with many of the positive traits of which you could identify, you will also recognize this person to exhibit the Three P's of success: Purpose, Poise and Passion. Now ask yourself, how do I present purpose, poise, and passion when I interact with others? Let's take a brief look at each of these characteristics.

Purpose: What is your purpose? What is your mission in life? Do you know where you want to be ten years from now, or even five years from now? If not, then take some time out to discover what would be your goal or purpose in life? Get together with individuals whom you respect and know well enough to help you identify answers to the above questions. In fact, you may wan to seek a professional coach who is trained to help you with your self discovery. Remember that without a clear destination it is quite difficult to decide what pathway you would want to travel to obtain your success. Even if five or ten years seem too far away to consider, think of where you want to be next year or the year thereafter. Once again, imagine a person you admire, in your own field or outside your professional arena, and you will realize that this person is able to communicate to others, implicitly or explicitly, a vision or a goal. This vision or goal is driven by a purpose which can be seen as the driving force that moves him/her forward.

Poise: An interesting phenomenon happens when you discover your purpose. You will find yourself going through life with greater calm, a composure if you will, that others will see in you. Poise is communicated by how you present yourself to others. You communicate poise by how you are able to provide eye contact with the people you talk to. You find yourself better able to genuinely listen to what other people have to say. When people are talking to you they feel a sense of who they are and what they are saying is important. Do you know anybody who gives you that sense of importance when talking to them? Imagine how this quality can aide you in your efforts to elicit support from others to help you achieve your goals, because those same people realize you are there to do the same for them!

Passion: Passion is having a career or a job that you enjoy. It is doing something which brings a sense of fulfillment and satisfaction to your life. You feel pride in what you do. Interestingly enough, when you have a purpose in life it is easy to feel the passion. Passion is believing that what you do matters. Passion is communicated by your words, your actions, and your body language. Once again, picture in your mind, an individual you know who is passionate about their endeavors. What does that person look like? How does that person sound? What is that person's voice inflection? Keep in mind, passion does not necessarily mean presenting a cheer or speech as you would find by a soccer or football coach. Passion is simply believing in what you do and presenting that belief in your behavior.

Listening

People with poise are good listeners. This same trait also applies to effective leaders. No matter what level on the career or organizational ladder you stand, you are there to help others achieve success. You cannot help others obtain their goals without knowing what is important to them. You learn what is important to others by being able to listen. One of the most crucial skills of communication is *active* listening. Active listening is the ability to respond to others in such a way as to let them know they have been heard and understood.

Think of yourself as a mirror when you are listening, reflecting a verbal image of what the person standing before you is saying. As a listener you observe the body language, facial expressions, and voice inflection, along with the content of what you hear. This gives you the total picture of both intent and the emotional state of the person speaking with you. The simplest form of active listening is paraphrasing. For example, if a customer says, "I am unhappy with the performance of this product," your reply might be, "you are disappointed with how this product works." Active listening is a deceptively simple but extremely effective tool that can create some amazing results.

Listed are some of the benefits you can accomplish through active listening:

- Empowerment: Through active listening you communicate to the other person that what they are saying is very important to you. This opens the door for that person to be more open to listening to what you have to say. You stand a better chance for your own ideas to be heard.

- Mutual respect: Active listening communicates respect and in turn the person to whom you are speaking will act accordingly.

- Improved working relationships: By developing the art of active listening and applying this skill appropriately, you will find people will be supportive and cooperative in their relationships with you.

- Improved confidence: As you feel greater cooperation and respect in your working relationships, so too will your confidence grow.

Regardless of the benefits of active listening, this skill is frequently overlooked or not utilized when it is needed the most. The following are some obstacles that keep people from utilizing active listening more often:

- Bad timing: You may be approached when you are in the middle of a project or your mind is preoccupied with other things. Consequently, you have difficulty listening. Take a break or offer a more appropriate time to talk when you know you can listen.

- Personal reaction: What you hear may be offensive to you or it may be something with which you strongly disagree. Remember, active listening is not agreeing but simply communicating that you understand what the other person is saying.

- You want desperately to be understood yourself: Consequently, you often jump in with your reactions or thoughts rather than letting the other person know he or she has been heard. Keep in mind active listening opens the doors for you to be heard as well.

- Confusing empathy with sympathy: You become hesitant to respond with active listening (empathy) for fear the other person may think you are agreeing with him/her. Sympathy is emotionally identifying with the other person. Empathy is simply expressing an understanding by viewing the situation from the shoes of the other person.

- Lack of training: Few people are natural at active listening, so training in this skill becomes a must. Learn to master the skill of active listening and you will find it will enhance your career and personal success. A good training program will help you learn the techniques and avoid the roadblocks. Keep in mind how good you feel when the person to whom you are speaking really understands what you are saying and use this knowledge to your benefit when communicating with others.

As you endeavor to achieve success in your personal and professional life, stop and take note of how you elicit the support and respect of the people you encounter. Whether these people are traveling upon the same road as you or simply crossing your path, the impact you have on their lives and the impact that they have on yours depends upon effective communication. Have an awareness of the Purpose, Poise and Passion that embraces your life and your work and how well you communicate this to others. Finally, remember we are social beings, and our ability to understand and be understood goes a long way toward developing successful and meaningful relationships.

Notes

Reference Checking

Honesty is the best policy

With the concern of corporate-scandal, many employers are finding it necessary to scrutinize the job candidate's background more closely in order to verify exactly who they are interested in hiring, and some companies are going beyond what had been considered the norm to accomplish this task.

A recent article published in The Wall Street Journal reported that during the year 2003 that 80% of employers surveyed had conducted criminal background checks on potential hires as compared to 51% in 1996, and 35% performed credit checks as compared to19% conducted that same year. Also, of the employers surveyed, seventy-nine percent verified the previous work history of candidates applying for top-level positions. In my experience, it is becoming more and more common for companies to request as many as ten work related references as compared to three that I was typically requested to check in previous years.

Understandably, there are a number of statistics to illustrate the need for a company to be extremely cautious. In the same article it was also reported that in the year 2002 there were more than 18,500 arrests for embezzlement in the U. S. alone. Additionally, an executive recruiting firm had found exaggerated or flat-out false information in 23% of over 7,000 executive resumes checked.

If you are an upper level executive, the scrutiny does not stop there. The Fair Credit Reporting Act allows credit checks on potential hires who will earn more than $75,000 per year.

Keep in mind that companies are not permitted by law to delve into your past without your permission, but in a tight market most job seekers are unlikely to risk refusing these background checks for fear of disqualifying themselves from a potential job offer.

Therefore, to help prevent you from being confronted with a potentially embarrassing or compromising situation:

- Examine your credit report periodically for possible errors.
- Be aware of what a potential employer may uncover before they do.
- Inform them of what they might find.
- Be completely honest.
- Be proactive if something negative were to be uncovered.

If you feel that you have been disqualified for a job because of an undesirable credit check, request that the employer foreword you a copy of the report (as required by law). Credit reporting agencies have been known to make mistakes, such as a shared first and last name but overlooked middle initial or social security number, or perhaps you have fallen victim to identity theft and were unaware. If you find an error on your report notify the employer immediately. It just may save your chances of being hired, and remember to always prepare your references to receive potential calls from prospective employers.

Notes

Negotiation of Salaries

Negotiating a salary should not propose a problem if you have prepared yourself beforehand. As a recruiter, I have never considered it advantageous for the employer and applicant to get into a haggling dispute over money. Therefore, prior to the interview I will always question the employer on what he/she is willing to pay. Typically, they would offer a salary range from a low to high dollar amount, and I would usually attempt to settle somewhere in the mid-range. It would be a big mistake for me to quote to the candidate the top dollar amount mainly because the employer does not want to initiate pay at the top of the position's salary range. What would they be able to offer as far as a salary increase in the near future unless they promote the individual to a higher paying position? On the part of the candidate, I will always operate from the minimum dollar amount that they would accept to start work. You might be thinking that this is not fair to the candidate, but understand that from a commissioned standpoint, it is to my advantage to obtain the highest dollar amount for the candidate as I can, but to be considered for hire, I also need the candidate to be as flexible on money as possible. Then, it becomes my job to negotiate a final starting salary, hopefully to the benefit of the employer and to the candidate.

If you are really concerned or hesitant about the proper way to conduct your own salary negotiations, you might want to hire an expert. Middle managers are learning what top executives have known for years, that hiring an expert adviser during job negotiations will often bring you a higher salary and perks package. They may also conduct role-playing sessions to help you in becoming more effective and at ease during salary discussions. These experts may be listed as pay coaches, lawyers, and compensation consultants. Their job is normally to research average salaries and compensation packages for a specific position in given industries. If you are not inclined to hiring a pay expert, there are alternative resources you may consider. Review data from the Bureau of Labor Statistics or download sites such as <u>Salary.com</u> which is a free database listing over 6,000 positions at different levels and fields. This site furnishes a low, middle, and high-range salary, along with a total compensation comparison. SalaryExpert.com (owned by a compensation specialist's firm) may also give you a reference on salaries and compensation packages. This information may also be discovered by consulting professional associations, business and trade periodicals, employment agencies, executive search firms, on-line salary surveys (as indicated above), career related websites, and job advertisements.

Keep in mind that employers have been dropping salaries for several years and are always interested in cutting overhead cost. It is very important to know your market value, especially if you have been out of the job market for some time. Given that you may not have a professional recruiter representing you, I offer some suggestions for you to follow in the negotiation of salary. Do not commit yourself on a dollar figure! Employers will always inquire as to what you were paid at your last position, and of course, this kind of determines what you may receive in the way of an offer, or what you would have in mind for a starting salary. If you answer with the minimum dollar amount, you risk settling for less than what may have been offered. If you ask for the top of the range, you risk not receiving an offer, for reason that they might feel that offering you a lower dollar amount would not be acceptable to you. When filling out the company's employment application leave the question of salary blank or just write "open". If the employer *asks* you what you are expecting in salary, just reply that if you are extended an offer you are sure that the offer would be fair and in line with your experience and qualifications and leave it at that. You may ask the employer what they are considering of as compensation for this level of the position, but leave the burden of salary on the employer and not on you. Once the offer has been made you can further negotiate if necessary, and at this point you will know that they want you to join the team and that they may be somewhat more flexible.

If you are relocating from one part of the country to another you should not expect the same salary that you were previously paid. The amount of compensation you may expect to receive may be at a higher or at a lower rate depending largely on the cost of living within that region. There are site references on the Internet that will give you salary comparisons and cost of living guidelines for given areas of the country. A helpful site that I have used for cost of living comparisons and salaries is:

Houseandhome.msn.com/pickaplace/comparecities.aspx.

When evaluating an offer, be sure to take into consideration the benefits, responsibilities, location, promotional aspects, and company environment. Know beforehand what you will need in the way of salary to live on and make that your minimum acceptable dollar amount. Once you have accepted the offer, ask for an offer letter confirming salary and benefits, (and when they become effective) job title, responsibilities, and the agreed upon start date.

Notes

Salaries Getting Lower

If at first you do succeed, try to hide your astonishment

In the last few years, I have observed that many employers are looking for quality employees but are not willing to pay the level of salaries that candidates have earned in their previous positions.

A recent article from the Wall Street Journal confirms this trend. According to a Bureau of Labor Statistics survey, 5.3 million workers were laid off from jobs they had held for at least three years between January 2001 and December 2003.

Average salaries for the re-employed workers fell by 16%. This decline in pay is the largest decline since the period between 1991 and 1993 when pay decreased by the same percentage. Professionals were also not immune from the income reduction. While 70% of the 800,000 displaced professionals found new jobs by January 2004, only half reported securing salaries equal to, or better than what they had previously earned. On average, salaries for professionals fell by about 14%. Managers felt an even greater blow in the pocketbook. Those displaced from financial management positions saw their paychecks shrink the most and suffered a decline by 17%.

We all know that the labor-market has been sluggish over the past few years, and a weak job market places the employer in the driver's seat. This becomes a paramount reason for candidates to develop confidence in negotiating a salary offer and to insure they not lose economic ground. The article further indicated that employers can sense that most unemployed professionals are basically afraid to negotiate for a higher salary in fear of losing a job opportunity. As a result, the candidate does not get the best offer for the position. To strengthen your negotiating position, continue to aggressively seek other job opportunities. The biggest mistake that people make when in serious discussions with an employer is to stop looking for other opportunities. You will be able to negotiate with more confidence if you know that you have other options.

Notes

Taking a Backward Step

There are times when it may become necessary to accept a position with less authority and responsibility. The answer to this question may depend on if you feel that the company that you plan on hiring into possesses some of the qualities that you would normally look for in a prospective employer. Some desired qualities might include job stability, personal or professional growth, culture, and career advancement potential. If so, then it may be worth the gamble. However, the downside to taking this direction is that you may find yourself fixed in a position that you cannot break out of. If you do find yourself in this scenario, it is best to approach the new job with a well-conceived plan for upward mobility, which always starts by performing well in the existing position. Keep in mind that it is still an initial opportunity to prove yourself. An outstanding performance will almost always catch the attention from higher ups.

While establishing yourself as a productive worker, elect to participate in committee assignments, cross-functional teams, and attend company social events to explore different areas and make and develop a wider contact base. You may even discuss your long term goals with your supervisor and enlist his/her support in branching out from your current position. If you are uncomfortable approaching your manager, you may need to create your own opportunities by developing a trusted network within the company. After all, you do have options by keeping your network and job search active but in a low profile.

Notes

Follow-Up

After your first or second interview always send a thank-you note by postal mail (not email) within two days following the interview. Address a brief letter to each of the people who interviewed you and thank them for their time spent with you. Express how much you enjoyed meeting them, and indicate your high level of interest in the position along with your desire to join their company. Declare that you would appreciate any further consideration given to you.

How long should you wait before contacting the employer? You do not want to become a "bother" to the employer by contacting them incessantly but if after a period of about ten days goes by and you have not heard from the interviewer, contact the hiring authority and once again thank him or her for taking the time to interview you. Express again your desire for the job, and ask if there are any additional questions or concerns about your background or qualifications. The interviewer may have some additional questions about your ability to perform some aspect of the job and this is the best time for you to overcome their concerns.

Following up your interview with a thank-you note and in keeping in touch with a phone call shows initiative and style. It is also an excellent opportunity to once again speak with the employer and re-establishes your name and qualifications into the mind of the hiring authority. He or she may have interviewed three or four additional people since your first visit, so it is important for you to stand out from the crowd and be more memorable than the other candidates. This is a continuation to sell yourself and overcome any doubts the hiring authority may have about hiring you.

It amazes me as to why people do not follow up with prospective employers after their initial interview. To me, it is just common courtesy. I have always insisted that my candidates follow up with a thank-you letter and a phone call. Again, **do not** leave a message on the interviewer's voice mail! If he or she is not available, continue trying until you can talk with them personally, or ask the company operator or secretary what would be a good time for you to reach them. You have already established yourself, but if you want to beat the competition, following up is a good way to do it.

Notes

Getting Older but Better

American businesses are finally becoming wiser and are hiring back much of its older workers, either for special projects or on a contractual basis. One of the fastest growing segments of temporary services is the need for retired or unemployed people with management experience. Many are hired for temporary assignments but soon find themselves in full time positions. During the late 1990's businesses were looking for ways to cut costs and believed that offering early retirement or eliminating certain key positions would be the answer. Consequently, the trend became to hire younger people with less experience and at reduced salaries. Now industry is finding out that in some cases, this trend may have been a short-sighted, and are coming to the conclusion that you just cannot replace highly skilled individuals having proven experience with people just learning the ropes. As a result, many of us in the older workforce are in demand again.

For financial and psychological reasons many of us are questioning the wisdom of taking full retirement, not only because of issues of personal fulfillment, but also because companies are now finding the need for people that possess irreplaceable skills, as well as individuals with strong work ethics. So what are the options? Well, you can follow this guide, conduct a job search, and hire on with a Consulting firm or a temporary placement office that offers management or technical assignments, or you can offer your services to an employer as a seasonal or even part time employee. There are many management and executive groups coming together to assist in finding jobs for their members. Recruiters like myself regularly send job descriptions for various positions to these groups for possible referrals. You may check with the Chamber of Commerce, Yellow pages, or the Internet for groups in your area. Some churches have also organized to offer this type of service.

Almost half of today's retirees feel a need to explore opportunities that may be available to them. If being a productive, employed person is still in your interest, go for it! You are not alone, many individuals previously considered past the retirement age are rejoining the work force, so why not you?

Notes

Your Terminated

If you don't like where you are, change it! You're not a tree

Brian Tracy

Difficult words to accept but understand this, it's not the end of the world its only if you make it so. I once interviewed a middle aged applicant who had worked in the engineering field for a number of years. When he sat down in my office his eyes were cast down and his shoulders were slumped. I ask him how I could help him and he said he needed a job and had looked everywhere for employment. I ask him what had happen to his last job as it appeared by his resume that he had worked for the same company for 7 years. He said he was fired and then proceeded to tell me what a miserable boss he had and what happen to him was an injustices and that the company was badly managed. As he went on it was oblivious to me why he was having a problem finding a new position. I ask him if he had discussed these things with potential employers and he said yes, then I ask him why? I had learned along time ago that an applicant should never under any circumstances bad mouth a previous employer and never vent bad experiences during an interview with a new potential employer. Don't bring up your termination if the interviewer doesn't know in advance, try keeping the interview positive. But if it's necessary to discuss it I'm giving you just one example as to what to say" My boss and I didn't agree on certain issues and he and I both decided that the job wasn't working out and the position wasn't the best fit for me and the company but I learned a lot and gained valuable knowledge working there" Being prepared before hand to answer a question of this sort is paramount to getting passed the issue and having a productive interview. Well getting back to my engineer I sent him out to talked with one of my clients for an engineering position. My client called me back after a couple of hours and said that he had just experienced the worst interview he's ever had. He said the applicant did nothing but talk about his previous employment and supervisor all in a negative manner. Well he had blown another opportunity by his negative attitude it was a real shame because the guy had excellent skills. I apologized to my client and waited for the applicant to call me. . He never did I guess he knew what he had done. Some people just seem to never learn.

The Key to interviewing is to stay positive no matter what. If you lost your last job by termination look to the bright side maybe it just wasn't the job for you maybe it didn't offer the challenge and the opportunity you would be happy with . As I indicated up to 75% of employed people are not truly satisfied with their current employment either because of low salary, no challenge or work environment. Find out what type of work and in what field would make you happy and challenged. If the new job requires more training or changing to another field then do it. Let's face facts you will spend a good percentage of your life working and the only way to be truly successful is doing what you like and enjoy. So being fired is not the end of the road. Take Russ Limbaugh he tells us that he was fired six or seven times and see where he is now.

Keep in mind that keeping positive and moving forward gets you the prize, as nothing else will.

Notes

Requesting a Pay Increase

The thought of asking your employer for an increase in salary often brings about feelings of insecurity and perhaps even anxiety, especially when the request comes at a time when the economy is somewhat sluggish and employment opportunities are reduced. According to the U. S. Department of Labor the year 2004 represented the fourth consecutive year where salary increases averaged less than 4%, and not much is expected to change in the foreseeable future. How then do you get more money for what you do, and how do you negotiate for a better salary increase than the industry average currently given? The answers usually will depend upon how prepared you are in defending your reason for asking, and also in how the request is made.

There are steps that you can take to prepare yourself to at least increase your confidence, and make the request more justifiable for the outcome that you are hoping to achieve. The following are very important things to know and to consider prior to your request for a pay increase:

Your Market Worth:

You will be able to negotiate from a stronger position if you know how your salary compares with those of others doing the same job, both within your company and your industry. In the chapter titled "Negotiation of Salaries" a couple of web-sites are listed as a resource for comparative salary information. These web-sites offer salary estimates, and are often derived from government data or employer surveys that tend to be low for public information. With this information serving as reference, you might consider widening your comparison by conducting your own investigation. For example, ask co-workers out to lunch and turn your conversation into a discussion about salary ranges for various positions, including your own. Join a professional organization, so that you can personally meet more people and gather additional information. Also, talk with professional recruiters, they typically know how people in your industry are being compensated and are normally willing to at least give you a position salary range. If you discover that your salary is lagging after completing your research, then make this a point during your discussion with your boss. Illustrate to him/her on how your salary is not stacking-up against others in your industry.

Your Value, or Lack of It:

A crucial point in your investigation should be to realize just how valuable you are considered to be by your present employer. Conduct an honest inventory of your contributions made, and if you find that you have little value and are not truly contributing, be thankful that you have not been fired and do not under any circumstance ask for a raise. I have seen far too many people who possess a "why me" mind-set, and are completely unaware of how un-productive an employee they are. Consider your last performance evaluation and what actions you have taken to address any problems or weaknesses. It is a must that you be completely honest with yourself. If you have not been performing well, this is again not the time to ask for a raise. However, if you find yourself to be a valued employee and staunch contributor, then you should have something to highlight. You should not expect to be recognized just for being a conscientious employee or a "hard-worker". Therefore, you may find it beneficial to talk with your boss and get his/her opinion on the value of your work performance. This information may give you the courage that you need to proceed to the next step. Document your achievements, such as money saving ideas, methods improvements, lucrative projects completed, and e-mails sent to you by superiors or clients congratulating you on a job well done. Prepare yourself to highlight these achievements when the time comes for negotiation.

Prepare for Negotiation:

Conventional wisdom instructs us to always ask for more money than we would be willing to settle for. Therefore, once you have made the decision on a desired dollar amount add another 10% to 20%. I would not recommend venturing much further beyond this amount because your request may lose credibility, and you also risk putting your employer on the defensive. If he/she dismisses your request with responses such as "money is tight" or "it's really not in the budget" or something of that sort, consider some alternatives, such as additional vacation time, an increase in your expense account, a laptop, or working from home a few days each month. Once you have determined which alternatives are really important to you, prioritize them and start from there. Skillful negotiators will use this approach nearly all of the time. For example, if you ask for a 10% raise but are willing to settle for 8%, be certain to include one or more of your alternatives to make the final sum agreed upon more desirable. A major bargaining tool is to have an outside offer for a better paying job, although I would not advise you to declare this at your initial request or meeting. Generally it is best to first "feel" your employer out for their views and opinions prior to the actual negotiation phase. However, sometimes it may become necessary to move out in order to move up. If you do have an outside offer, be prepared to submit a resignation if you do not get what you believe is deserved. On the other hand, if you do not have an outside job offer, **do not** say that you do. This is not the time for bluffing.

How to Conduct the Meeting:

Begin the discussion with a request for a salary increase, a desired dollar amount, and an explanation as to why you deserve it. This is where a written list of your accomplishments is helpful. If you have also done your research on comparative salary levels and how your salary contrasts with others, then naming a dollar figure should not propose a problem. By being the first to name a figure, you will have established a starting point as opposed to letting your employer establish the range. Listen attentively to their response, and keep in mind that the best negotiators do not necessarily have the best argument, but they will routinely pick up on what's really being said. Therefore, the key is to really listen and ask relevant questions, such as what additional achievements would be required, or why a raise would not be possible at this time. Allow your employer to answer and consider your responses very carefully. Keep in mind that 85%-90% of communication is nonverbal. Pay close attention to the body language of your boss as well as your own. Again as discussed in previous chapters for conducting yourself in an interview setting, pay close attention to your posture during this time. You should be sitting forward in your seat, with your arms and legs uncrossed to demonstrate that you are not presenting a challenge.

Keep steady eye contact and smile. In contrast, if your boss takes the position of crossed arms, etc., this may very well indicate to you that he/she is not being receptive to what you are saying. In that case, rescheduling the meeting might be better for all concerned. It could be possible that they may just be in a bad mood or having a rough day. Although you should be prepared to hear an abrupt refusal this is not the time to give up. Attempt to keep the conversation going by discussing your alternatives in lieu of an immediate pay increase, or requesting when would be a more favorable time to discuss the matter further. Take notes during your meeting to use as reference material should the need arise to conduct an additional meeting. Attempt to close the meeting without anyone suffering hard feelings, regardless of the outcome. If you do not receive the desired amount, ask your boss what would be necessary on your part to be considered for the pay increase that you have requested. Again, listen carefully to his/her response, and then consider whether or not you are willing to do what is required to reach the amount that you desire.

Excerpts taken from an article on *"Asking for a salary increase"* published in *The Career Journal*

Notes

Conclusion

"It is wise to keep in mind that neither success nor failure is ever final." Roger Babson

Finding a job is not easy to say the least. It does not matter if you are just starting your career, or a seasoned veteran who has not had to look for a job in many years. The challenges that you encounter can be very disheartening. I hope this information has been helpful to you. Historically, the job-market has rarely ever been easy for those searching for employment and I am especially concerned for the individual who has worked for the same company over a number of years and suddenly has lost his or her job. Never the less, the key is to be persistent, set goals for yourself, and never give up. If you apply at least some of the principles that are outlined in this publication, hopefully, they will make finding a job that much easier. Believe me, I have placed hundreds of candidates using these same principals. Job hunting can be made a little easier and much more effective if you develop a plan and stick to it. The problem that many people have is that they do not know how or where to begin their job search, or with whom. Use my tips to assist you to prepare, get organized, and develop your action plan.

- Make an inventory list of your skills and accomplishments using the Skills Inventory Worksheet. This list will enlighten you as to what natural skills you possess, and from those skills which ones you most enjoy doing. Continue to add to and to refine your list as you continue to grow.

- Construct your resume using the Three Steps to Writing Effective Resumes as a guide. Keep in mind that you may have to refine it to include the buzz words and experiences outlined in the employer's job description. Generic resumes will not get anyone noticed. Remember, your resume should be written to match the employer's needs. Depending upon the level of position that you are seeking, always be as truthful and honest as you can.

- Make a list of your friends to use as referrals. Find out where they work and what they do.

- Make a list of companies that you would like to work for and the reasons why. Research those companies so that you completely understand what they do. Make up a cover letter specialized for each company indicating your interest and how you feel that you can contribute to their organization. Try to get the name of a manager in charge of the department that you would be qualified for and interested in. Address the cover letter directly to his or her attention and not to the personnel department.

- Contact your previous employer's competitors and suppliers. They may be in of need your skills and experience since you are already familiar with their industry and operations.

- Continue to expand your personal referral and company lists. Set your weekly goals as to how many contacts you want to make in a given week. Keep track of the results of your efforts and always continue to improve your search techniques.

- Use the worksheets and forms provided at the end of this book to keep record of your generated data.

- Be flexible on salary requirements. Sometimes moving up requires taking a step back.

The economy and job market conditions fluctuate with time. I can honestly say that there is a light at the end of the tunnel. Just keep reassuring yourself that you will do it, and further more, never give up!

Please write to me and let me know when you land that terrific job. I sincerely hope that this book will help guide you in conducting your job search. Also, keep in mind that in some business climates, we may have to look at *every* job, and conclude that it may be just temporary. With all of the outsourcing, downsizing, plant closings, and uncontrolled instabilities, no one can guarantee the future. Consequently, we must not look at all jobs as permanent and offering longevity as was perhaps realized by our parents and grandparents. Changing and moving to new fields is not all bad and as they say, "diversity is the spice of life."

Now, that you possess the secrets of the trade, give it your best shot!!

Good luck and happy hunting!
Darrell Laughlin
dlaughlin@cinci.rr.com

Appendix
Worksheets and Forms

Appendix A
Skills Inventory

During your previous work history, you have developed certain skills and/or aptitudes. If you are interested in changing your career field or remaining in your current occupation, many of these skills may be transferable. Refresh yourself on these skills because you may need them for possible discussions during an interview. For example, you may be learning and implementing a new computer program, learning to use different types of production equipment, or selling products to other businesses, etc.

List as many of the skills that you have acquired during various work experiences.

1.
2.
3.
4.
5.
6.
7.
8.
9.
10.
11.
12.

Of the skills that you listed, highlight those that you enjoy doing. These are the skills that you will want to focus on during your job search.

Of the skills that you feel that you have a natural talent and/or ability place a "T" after each. These are also the skills that you will want to focus on during your search.

Appendix B
Company Research

Use this worksheet to summarize your research on companies that you have targeted, or companies that you have interviews scheduled.

Company Name: _____ Website: _____

Address: _____ Phone: _____

City, State, ZIP: _____ Industry: _____

Referral name (if any):

Company Information:

History, growth, size:

Manufacturing or Service:

Competitors/suppliers:

Type of clientele:

Hiring/management contacts:

Possible needs:

Notes:

Appendix C
Referral List

Your referrals are the most important aspect in your networking program. List all friends, acquaintances, previous co-workers, members of your associations, past supervisors, and individuals that you know who work with competing industries. Continually add to this list, referrals that you receive from individuals that you have contacted. Keep asking "Who do you know?" "Who do they work for?" and "What is their title and work number?" **Always ask permission to use their name as a referral.**

Name: Company: Title: Work number:

Referred by:
_____

Name: Company: Title: Work number:

Referred by:
_____

Name: Company: Title: Work number:

Referred by:
_____

Name: Company: Title: Work number:

Referred by:
_____

Name: Company: Title: Work number:

Referred by:
_____

Appendix D
Weekly Activities

Record your various job search activities for a given week. This list will assist you in your planning and scheduling efforts, and also give you an indication as to what areas you should focus more time on.

Week of:

Activities	Mon	Tue	Wed	Thur	Fri	Letters	Results/Comments
Networking							
Friends/ Assoc.							
Associations							
Company Referrals							
Alumni							
Business Associates							
Recruiter Contacts							
Classified Advertising							
Job boards Internet							
Job fairs							
Employer calls							
Letters sent to Employers							

Follow-up calls							
Interviews							

Appendix E
Personal Interview Follow-up

Company: _____ Position: _____ Date: _____

Interview number: First   Second   Third

Interviewed with:

Initial comments about interview:

Time spent with person conducting interview:

Position discussed:

Questions asked by interviewer:

Was career opportunity/advancement potential discussed?

Your feelings about the opportunity:

What questions did you ask?

Did you ask for the job?

Was a second interview scheduled?

How does this interview compare with others?

Did you receive additional leads/contacts?

Was salary discussed? If yes, give details.

Was benefits package discussed? If yes, give details.

If job is offered are you ready to accept? If no, give details.

Did you discuss when you could begin work?

Were references requested? If yes, whom did you list?

Have you informed these references to expect a call?

How was interview ended?

Printed in the United States
105455LV00003B/187-195/P